DATE DUE

Jul 9 83			
Aug 13 '84			

Tales from Russia. By Marie J. Garczynska.
    Silver Burdett [c1976]
    124p. illus. (World folktale library)

1. FOLKLORE — RUSSIA   I. Garczynska, Marie J
II. Series

2/15

THE WORLD FOLKTALE LIBRARY

Tales from Russia

By Marie-J. Garczynska

Illustrated by Marie Chartrain

SILVER BURDETT COMPANY

Morristown, New Jersey
Glenview, Ill. • *Palo Alto* • *Dallas* • *Altanta*

© Librairie Hachette, 1976
Adapted and published in the United States by Silver Burdett Company,
Morristown, N. J. 1981 Printing

Library of Congress Catalog Card Number: 80-52512   ISBN 0-382-06597-2

CONTENTS

Prince Ivan and the Firebird

Once upon a time there was a czar who was called Vladimir. Czar Vladimir owned a most beautiful orchard near his palace. In the middle of this orchard grew a truly extraordinary tree. It was an apple tree that bore golden apples all summer and all winter. This wonderful tree was famous throughout Russia.

One day the czar decided to count all the golden apples on the tree. There were one hundred and thirteen apples! The czar, who had a very good memory, did not forget this number, and he came back the next morning to count his apples again. Great was his astonishment when he discovered that now there were only one hundred and twelve of them!

Czar Vladimir thought that his orchard was well guarded and that none of his subjects would dare take a single piece of his fruit. So who could possibly have come to steal his golden apples? The czar was determined to find out!

When the sun had set, Czar Vladimir put on a large cape that was the color of night and went himself to stand guard in the orchard.

The moment the czar began to feel sleepy, he saw something that looked like a flash of fire pass in front of his eyes. He looked again and saw a marvelous bird with golden plumage and luminous eyes flying through the orchard.

It perched for a moment on the apple tree and with its beak it plucked a golden apple from a branch and disappeared with it into the sky.

All this happened so fast that the czar did not have time to move. And the bird was so strange and so dazzling that Czar Vladimir asked himself if he had been dreaming. He had certainly never seen such a bird before. But since the golden apples shone even in the night, the czar had no difficulty counting them again. Now there were only one hundred and eleven apples!

Czar Vladimir went home to bed, but he was not able to fall asleep for a long time. He lay in his bed thinking about his strange experience and about the mysterious golden bird.

As soon as it was morning, he called before him his three young sons—Dimitri, Vassili, and Ivan.

"Brave sons," he said to them, "I have seen with my own eyes, coming from heaven or from hell, a truly marvelous bird—a bird of gold and fire! It comes in the night to my orchard, perches on my magic apple tree, and takes one of my golden apples away. To the one of you three who brings that bird back alive, I will give half of my empire and half of all my riches, for I want this firebird to keep in a cage in my palace.

"Your Majesty," said Prince Dimitri, who was the eldest, "let me stand guard in your orchard this evening. I will bring the firebird back to you!"

As soon as night fell, Prince Dimitri put on his cape that was the color of night and went to stretch out under a tree in the orchard. He had taken a large net with him to capture the

wondrous bird. But while watching the stars twinkle, Prince Dimitri fell sound asleep.

The firebird came flying into the orchard, picked a golden apple, and disappeared into the night. No one saw it, but when the czar walked in his orchard the next morning and counted his apples, there were only one hundred and ten!

The czar called for his son. "Prince Dimitri," he said to him, "did you not see the firebird come into my orchard last night?"

"Your Majesty," answered Dimitri, "I watched all night and the bird did not come. I am sorry, for I would have wished to bring it back to please you."

What Dimitri really wanted was to possess half of all his father's wealth!

Czar Vladimir was astonished by his son's reply, for he knew that another apple was missing. But to Prince Dimitri he said only, "Tonight Prince Vassili shall stand guard, for I must have this bird of gold and fire!"

In his turn, Prince Vassili put on his cape that was the color of night, took a large net, and went to his father's orchard to capture the wondrous bird.

He stretched out under a tree and waited. But the night was so calm, the hours so long, and the stars in the sky so numerous, that he, too, fell sound asleep.

At that very moment the firebird came, picked an apple, and disappeared into the night. No one saw it, but when the czar walked in his orchard the next day and counted his apples, there were only one hundred and nine!

Back in his palace, the czar called for his second son. "Prince Vassili," he asked him, "did you not see the firebird come into my orchard last night?"

"Your Majesty," answered Vassili, who did not hesitate to lie, just as his older brother had, "I watched the whole night, and I can assure you that the bird did not come. I am very sorry, for I would have brought it back to please you."

What Vassili really wanted was to possess half of all his father's wealth!

The czar was astonished by this reply, for he knew that another golden apple was missing. But he simply said, "This evening it will be Prince Ivan's turn to stand guard, for I want this bird of gold and fire for my palace!"

The third night Ivan, the youngest son, put on his cape that was the color of night, and went to guard his father's orchard.

Since he was determined not to fall asleep, Ivan did not stretch out under a tree. Instead he sat down and watched the tree with the one hundred and nine golden apples that shone in the dark.

One hour passed, then two, then three. Ivan kept looking at the golden apples in order not to fall asleep. As the last stroke of midnight rang out from the palace belfry, a bright flash passed before Prince Ivan's tired eyes and suddenly the entire orchard lit up brightly!

Prince Ivan arose, astounded. He stared at the firebird, which had just appeared and perched in the apple tree. The

moment the bird was about to fly away again, taking an apple with him, Ivan seized it by its tail feathers. But the bird, with supernatural strength, freed itself, and with a single flap of its powerful wings, flew away once again with a golden apple! Astonished, Ivan watched it leave. When it had disappeared in the east and lost itself among the stars, Ivan noticed that he still held one of the golden feathers in his hand.

As soon as morning came, Prince Ivan gave the golden tail feather to his father and told him about the peerless bird and about everything that had happened.

The young prince then asked Czar Vladimir to give him Vostok, his favorite horse, for he wanted to go in search of the firebird. He promised his father that he would not rest until he had brought the marvelous bird back to the palace.

At that moment the princes Dimitri and Vassili felt jealousy pinch their hearts. Not only had their young brother given their father a wonderful golden feather as bright as fire, but if he found the fabulous bird and brought it back to their father, he would be given half of the empire and half of all the riches of the czar.

However Dimitri and Vassili were not courageous enough to set forth in pursuit of the firebird themselves. They remained at the palace, their hearts full of spitefulness, while Prince Ivan was already galloping towards the east.

Ivan rode for three days and three nights in the direction in which he had seen the bird disappear. On the morning of the fourth day, he found himself at the crossing of several roads. His horse suddenly reared up in front of a sign on which Ivan could read

> The one who goes straight ahead will be
> hungry and thirsty and will die!
> The one who goes to the right will live
> but will lose his horse!
> The one who goes to the left will die
> but his horse will live!

Ivan did not hesitate. He knew that he must sacrifice his horse and continue his search. Therefore he turned towards the right. He rode on for three more days, stopping only to sleep, drink some water from the streams, and eat a few dry cakes that he had brought with him.

As he was riding through the deep forest, he saw an enormous gray wolf, which came out of the bushes and said to him, "Prince Ivan, why have you come here? Did you not see the sign?"

"Gray Wolf, since you know who I am, you must also know that I promised my father, Czar Vladimir, to bring back to him the bird of gold and fire who is carrying off the golden apples from his orchard."

At that very instant the gray wolf returned to the bushes and Ivan's horse fell dead on the spot! The prince was very grieved, for Vostok was the faithful companion who had tirelessly shared this strange adventure with him. However Ivan, remembering the promise he had made to his father, bravely started out on his journey once again.

He had been walking for three days, when the gray wolf again came out of the bushes to confront him.

"Prince Ivan," said the wolf, "I am sorry about the death of your horse. I can see that you are a very brave man, and I am going to help you. Jump on my back and I will take you wherever you wish to go."

Prince Ivan did not hesitate. He jumped on the gray wolf's back and said to him, "You know that I am looking for the firebird. Take me to it for I promised my father that I would bring the fabulous bird back to him."

"Do not fear, I will take you to it," answered the gray wolf. And he bounded through the woods all day long, faster than the best horse from the stables of the czar. It was dark when the gray wolf finally stopped at the foot of a high, thick wall.

"Climb this wall, Prince Ivan," said the wolf. "On the other side are the gardens of Prince Petrov. The firebird is there in a golden cage hanging from the branch of a maple tree. Take the bird, but be very careful not to take down the cage."

Prince Ivan scaled the high wall easily. As soon as he was in the gardens of Prince Petrov his heart jumped for joy as he recognized the glittering firebird. He opened the cage and took the bird, who came willingly. He was just about to go back over the wall, when he said to himself, "That cage of gold is truly beautiful. I really do not want to leave it behind. Also, how will I bring the bird back to my father if it isn't in a cage?" And he reached out to take the cage.

But hardly had he touched the golden cage, when all the little bells that were attached to it started to chime, awakening everyone in Prince Petrov's palace! Immediately lights went on all over the palace. Guards ran through the garden and seized Prince Ivan, who had to give up the bird. The guards brought Ivan into the palace where Prince Petrov was waiting.

"Young man," scolded the prince in a severe voice, "this golden bird belongs to me. Who gave you permission to come into my garden to take it away? But first of all, who are you? And where do you come from?"

"Sir, I am Ivan, the third son of Czar Vladimir. Your firebird comes at night to my father's orchard and steals his golden apples. My father has sent me to look for this bird. I promised to bring it back to him alive whatever the difficulties I might encounter!"

"Prince Ivan," answered Prince Petrov, "I must admit that you are courageous. But if you had simply come and asked me for the firebird, I would have given it to you. However, since you tried to steal it from me, I will pardon you only if you do something extraordinary for me!

"At the other end of the world, in the kingdom of Czar Afron, there gallops a horse with a mane of gold. If you succeed in bringing it back to me, I promise to give you my firebird."

Prince Ivan sadly left the palace, not knowing in which direction to go. But the gray wolf was waiting for him nearby.

"Prince Ivan," he said to him, "Prince Ivan, why did you not listen to me?"

"Gray Wolf, my friend," answered the young man, "the gold of the cage dazzled me and I forgot what you had told me."

"Jump on my back once again," ordered the wolf. "I will take you where you must go." And for three days Prince Ivan rode on the swift gray wolf. Finally his strange mount stopped in front of Czar Afron's stables.

"Prince Ivan, listen to me very closely this time," advised the wolf. "Go into the stable, take the horse with the golden mane, but do not touch anything else. Remember that Prince Petrov wants only the horse with the golden mane!"

The doors of the stable were half open. Prince Ivan entered without a sound and found all the grooms asleep. The wondrous horse with the mane of gold seemed to be waiting for him. The prince was about to lead him away, when his eyes fell on the most extraordinary reins hanging on the wall. They were made of solid gold!

"They are so beautiful!" he said to himself. "And they would be so useful to me for leading the horse with the golden mane back to Prince Petrov."

But the moment he touched the golden reins, all the grooms awoke. They seized Prince Ivan before he had time to move and brought him before their master, Czar Afron.

"Young man," exclaimed Czar Afron in a formidable voice, "the horse with the golden mane belongs to me. Who gave you permission to come into my stables? But first of all, who are you? And where do you come from?"

"Sir, I am the third son of Czar Vladimir. I had been searching for the firebird that stole the golden apples from my father's orchard. And I found that wonderful bird in the gardens of Prince Petrov. Prince Petrov promised me the firebird if I bring him your horse with the golden mane."

"Prince Ivan, if you had asked me for my horse with the mane of gold, I would willingly have given it to you for Prince

Petrov. But since you tried to rob me, I can pardon you only if you do something truly extraordinary for me!

"At the other side of great Russia lives Ludmilla the Beautiful, the one I love! If you succeed in finding her and bringing her to me, I will give you my horse with the mane of gold and the golden reins."

Prince Ivan sadly left Czar Afron's palace, not knowing in which direction to go. But the wolf was waiting for him nearby. "Prince Ivan," he said to him, "Prince Ivan, why don't you ever listen to me?"

"Gray Wolf," answered the desolate man, "please excuse me! Those golden reins so dazzled me that I forgot what you told me. But can you help me once more? I must go to the other end of great Russia to find Ludmilla the Beautiful for Czar Afron who wants to marry her."

"I know," answered the gray wolf. "Jump on my back and I will take you where you must go."

And Prince Ivan rode on the back of the gray wolf for three more days. At dawn on the fourth day, the wolf stopped in front of a gate made entirely of gold.

"This time," said the wolf, "it is I who will go look for Ludmilla the Beautiful, for I know that you will once again be dazzled! Wait for me under this big elm tree!"

Prince Ivan was very tired from his long ride. He leaned against the tree and fell asleep as soon as the wolf had disappeared.

Suddenly the voice of the wolf made him jump up with a start, "Quick, Prince Ivan! Wake up and jump on my back behind Ludmilla!"

Prince Ivan bounded to his feet and jumped on the grey wolf who did not even take time to stop. He ran with his stomach close to the ground, fast as the wind, carrying Ludmilla the Beautiful and Prince Ivan on his back.

Now the young prince could not keep his eyes from Ludmilla. She was the most beautiful girl he had ever seen! "Gray

Wolf, do not hurry so!" he exclaimed over and over. He did not want his ride with the lovely Ludmilla to end too quickly.

But the gray wolf seemed to hear nothing, and all three soon arrived at the gates of the kingdom of Czar Afron. At that moment, Prince Ivan felt that he would die if he were separated from Ludmilla the Beautiful.

"What is the matter, Prince Ivan?" asked the wolf. "You seem so unhappy."

"Gray Wolf, my friend," answered the young man, "why should I not be sad enough to die at the thought of exchanging Ludmilla the Beautiful, whom I already love, for a horse with mane and reins of gold, which means nothing to me?"

"Trust me, Prince Ivan, and do exactly what I ask of you. We are going to leave Ludmilla the Beautiful in these birch woods, and you and I will go to the palace of Czar Afron."

Prince Ivan did not understand, but he went with the gray wolf up to the door of the palace and boldly entered. Just as Czar Afron came to greet them, the gray wolf changed himself into a lovely young girl exactly like Ludmilla the Beautiful!

"Prince Ivan," said the czar, "you have earned my horse with the mane and reins of gold. Take it — and happy journey!"

Whereupon the prince jumped into the saddle and galloped like the wind towards the birch woods to find the real Ludmilla who was waiting for him. He seated her on his horse with the golden mane and they started out together for the kingdom of Prince Petrov.

Suddenly Prince Ivan was filled with remorse as he thought of his faithful friend, the gray wolf, whom he had forgotten for a while.

"Gray Wolf, what happened to you?" he called. At once the gray wolf came out of the bushes, and Ivan happily jumped on his back, leaving Ludmilla the Beautiful to ride the horse with the mane of gold. The two mounts galloped swiftly side by side towards the kingdom of Prince Petrov.

"Gray Wolf, do not hurry so!" Ivan began to plead as soon as

he saw the roof of the palace standing out clearly on the horizon.

"But why?" questioned the gray wolf.

"Friend Wolf," answered the young man, "do you not see that only this horse with the golden mane is worthy of Ludmilla the Beautiful? How can I possibly exchange it for a bird of gold and fire, no matter how wondrous?"

"Trust me, Prince Ivan, and above all, do exactly what I ask of you. We are going to leave Ludmilla the Beautiful and the horse with the golden mane in this little grove of fir trees. We two are going to the palace of Prince Petrov."

Once again Prince Ivan followed the gray wolf without understanding. And the moment they entered the palace, the young man saw the wolf change himself into a wonderful horse with a mane and reins of gold, exactly like the one Ludmilla the Beautiful was riding.

"Prince Ivan," said Prince Petrov, "you have earned the firebird and the golden cage. I give them to you!"

Immediately the prince returned to the grove of fir trees, carrying the bird in its golden cage. The princess and the horse with the golden mane were waiting for him. He took Ludmilla up before him on the wonderful horse and, holding the firebird in its cage, flew as fast as the wind towards the palace of his father, Czar Vladimir.

Suddenly Prince Ivan was overcome with remorse. He had just remembered his faithful old friend, the gray wolf, whom in his happiness he had again forgotten.

"Gray Wolf," he called, "what has happened to you?"

Then the gray wolf came out of the bushes once again and stood before him.

"Jump on my back," the wolf said to him. "I will take you where you must go."

"This time," answered Prince Ivan, "we shall return to my father's palace. I am going to introduce him to Ludmilla, my beautiful one, and give him the firebird! I thank you Gray

Wolf, my friend. Without your help my courage would not have been enough."

They started out again and after they had been travelling for many hours, the gray wolf stopped at exactly the spot in the woods where the horse Vostok had fallen dead.

"Prince Ivan, you no longer need your friend Gray Wolf. You can continue your journey mounted on your faithful horse, Vostok!"

And with those words the gray wolf disappeared into the bushes and Vostok bounded out of a thicket! Prince Ivan, happy to have his horse again, jumped on its back and started to gallop joyously at the side of his beloved Ludmilla.

It was not long before they found themselves in the kingdom of Czar Vladimir. When they were no more than twenty leagues from the palace, they decided to rest for a moment in the forest. They dismounted, tied their horses to the trunk of a birch tree, and carefully hung the golden cage holding the firebird on a branch.

While Ivan and Ludmilla were speaking together of their strange adventure, the sound of galloping hooves startled them. Almost immediately two horsemen appeared. They were Dimitri and Vassili, Prince Ivan's older brothers. The brothers fell into each other's arms and embraced affectionately.

But when the two older ones saw the firebird in its golden cage, the wondrous horse, and Ludmilla the Beautiful, jealousy so filled their hearts that there was no longer room for love of Prince Ivan!

They jumped on Ivan, tied him to the trunk of a tree, and seized all he possessed—Ludmilla the Beautiful, the firebird, the horse with the golden mane, and faithful Vostok. Then they fled through the woods, paying no attention to the cries of Ludmilla nor the pleas of Prince Ivan.

"Listen to me, Princess," warned Dimitri, "you are in our power and if you try to escape, you will die! Here is the sword

that will kill you if you do not tell our father, Czar Vladimir, that you, as well as the firebird and the horse with the golden mane, are our rightful conquest."

The other wicked brother added, "Our father has promised half his empire and half of all his wealth to the son who brings the firebird back alive. We are going to tell our father that Prince Ivan is dead, and then we will be rich and powerful!" And they continued on their wild gallop through the forest, dragging Ludmilla the Beautiful with them.

All this time Prince Ivan struggled alone in the woods, trying to free himself so that he might fly to the rescue of his beloved. Unable to loose his bonds, he was soon suffering from hunger and thirst. At the end of three days and three nights, the crows gathered in the branches above him, awaiting his death.

Then the gray wolf, who had long been hoping that Dimitri and Vassili would abandon their evil plans, came out of the bushes and approached Prince Ivan. But poor Ivan could no longer recognize his friend.

"Crows!" the gray wolf called. "Come quickly and help me free Prince Ivan or he will die!"

"But Sir Wolf, we have been waiting for his death for three days and three nights!"

"If you do not help me," shouted the gray wolf, "I will not leave a single crow alive in all the forests of Russia!"

Then all the crows quickly came down from the tree and started to pick with their sharp beaks at the ropes holding the prince. The ropes gave way at last and Prince Ivan fell to the ground unconscious.

"And now," ordered the gray wolf, "go get me some water."

It was thus, thanks to the gray wolf and with the help of all the crows of the forest, that Prince Ivan's life was saved.

"Prince Ivan," the gray wolf said when Ivan opened his eyes, "there is not a second to lose. Your brothers lied to your father, and Vassili is about to marry Ludmilla, who is helpless to defend herself. Jump on my back and I will carry you to your father's palace." And in two bounds they were at the gates of the palace.

"This time you do not need me, Prince Ivan," the gray wolf said. "I wish you much happiness."

The prince thanked the gray wolf a hundred times over and went into the palace. Of course no one was expecting him because his brothers, with false tears, had reported his death.

He burst into the great hall just as Czar Vladimir had seated himself at the engagement feast. At the czar's right was Ludmilla the Beautiful with Prince Vassili beside her. And at the czar's left sat the other wicked brother, Prince Dimitri.

As soon as she saw Ivan, the princess rushed to throw herself into his arms and exclaimed, "Here is my prince—the one who conquered my heart, the one who brought back the firebird for Czar Vladimir, the one who gave me the horse with the golden mane!"

The czar embraced his son, whom he had thought he would never see again, and asked him to tell the story of his extraordinary adventures. Everyone was having such a happy time that it was a long while before anyone noticed that Vassili and Dimitri had disappeared. After the wicked things they had done, no one was sorry that they had gone, and the celebration went on.

That very evening Prince Ivan married his princess, Ludmilla the Beautiful. They lived happily together for many years, and neither of them ever forgot the gray wolf.

Soldier Fedor's Card Game

Fedor the soldier had served his country and his czar faithfully for twenty long years. At the end of this period he received his discharge and his pay. He was not rich, but he was free!

Since he had neither wife nor house, Fedor decided to travel around the world. Later he would choose the wife who would please him and by then he would have found himself work and a home.

Soldier Fedor traveled for a long time, saw the world as he wished, and calmly spent the few rubles that made up his fortune.

One day, when he had only three crackers left in the bottom of his knapsack, he met a beggar on the road. The beggar was ill and asked him for alms. Without hesitating, Fedor gave him a cracker, keeping the other two for himself.

A little later, he met a second beggar. After greeting him, this beggar, too, asked him for alms. Fedor had only two crackers left, but he did not hesitate to give the beggar one, keeping the last one for himself.

But towards evening, along came a third beggar. He was an old man with long silver hair and a long white beard. He seemed exhausted and terribly poor. This time Fedor hesitated. He said to himself, "If I give him my last cracker, I will have nothing left! But if I only give him half of the cracker, he might meet the other two beggars, who have each received a whole cracker, and will be hurt! I am going to give him the whole cracker! I am young; I will find a way to get along."

Fedor then gave his last cracker to the old man, who accepted it gladly. Picking up his knapsack, which was now entirely empty, Fedor was about to start on his way again, when the old man began to speak to him, "Tell me, brave soldier, what can I give you to thank you? What do you need? What can I do for you?"

"God keep me from asking you for anything, kind old man! I have given you the little I had, but I do not wish anything in exchange!" exclaimed Fedor.

"Just the same, tell me what would please you, for I really want to thank you," insisted the old man.

"Very well! If you have a deck of cards, give it to me; that would please me," said Fedor.

The old man took a deck of cards out of his beggar's sack and held it out to Fedor, saying, "Here, take it, and with it I give you the power always to win, wherever you may be and whoever the players might be!"

Fedor put the pack of cards in his knapsack, thanked the old man, and started on his way again. But the old man stopped him once more.

"Brave soldier, take this bag as well to remember me by. It will serve you all your life. If by chance you meet a rabbit or bird or whatever you may wish to put in there, you have only to open the bag and repeat—

Hop quick! Hop quack!
You must enter
into the sack!

—and the rabbit or the bird or whatever you want will go right into the bag!"

"Thank you," said the soldier, and he took the sack and started off.

After walking for a while, he came to the edge of a pond where three wild geese were swimming. The soldier said to himself gaily, "By Jove, Fedor, this is the moment to try your sack!"

He took the bag off his shoulder, opened it wide, and said—

Hop quick! Hop quack!
Come on, geese,
into the sack!

Hardly had he finished saying these words, when the three wild geese flew straight into the sack! The soldier quickly buckled his bag, adjusted it on his shoulder, and went on his way.

In the evening, Fedor came to a city where he had never been before, and headed directly for the inn. Upon entering, he took the geese out of his bag and said to the owner, "Innkeeper, take this goose and have it roasted for me. For your trouble I will give you the second goose. As for the third goose, I would gladly trade it for a loaf of bread and a pitcher of good wine."

The innkeeper agreed to the bargain, and soon everything was prepared. Before long, soldier Fedor, seated in the large room of the inn, was happily eating his nice fat goose, accompanied by some good wine and a loaf of bread. He had not realized how very hungry he was!

As he was partaking of this plentiful meal, he noticed a

magnificent palace directly across from the inn. He got up and went over to the window, the better to admire it.

The palace was built entirely of rose-colored marble. Its roofs were of glazed tile and its cupolas were covered with gold. But this wondrous palace seemed absolutely deserted, and all its windowpanes were broken.

"Could a thunderbolt have struck that building, breaking all its windows and causing the inhabitants to flee?" he asked the innkeeper.

"You must know, brave soldier," answered the innkeeper, "that our king had this palace built for himself and his family. No one knows how it happened, but, unhappily, Satan and his entire company of devils took possession of the palace instead. This palace is haunted, and our king has never been able to live in it. Each night for the last ten years, an army of demons has held revels there with all the devils of hell. There is dancing and screaming and fighting and card playing. In the

morning, the demons take their deviltries elsewhere and all becomes silent again. But each night they return again to the palace."

While the innkeeper was talking, soldier Fedor had an idea. He immediately had himself brought before the king and said to him, "Your Majesty, grant me permission to pass one single night in your deserted palace."

"Deserted! At midnight tonight it will not be deserted! I can see that you are not from these parts, brave soldier. Haven't they told you that all those who, like yourself, wanted to spend a night in the palace, never came out alive? No, I will not let you lose your life for this palace that the devils have taken from me!"

"But, Your Majesty, I am a Russian soldier! I fear neither fire nor death nor demons! I went into battle for my God and my czar and I did not die! Do you believe, Your Majesty, that I will lose my life just by spending a night in your palace?"

"I repeat, brave soldier—the palace is no longer mine, but Satan's. He who enters it in the evening does not come out of it alive. What can one Russian soldier do against all the assembled devils and their evils?"

But soldier Fedor persisted so strongly in his resolve, that the king finally said to him, "If you do not value your life, go ahead, then, since you want to so badly!"

So Fedor took all he possessed—his soldier's knapsack, his sword, his magic bag, and his deck of cards—and entered the haunted palace of the king. At that hour the palace was completely deserted; all the demons were away about their wicked business.

The noise of the soldier's ironclad boots echoed ominously through the empty rooms of the palace, but Fedor paid no attention. He intended to spend the night in the most beautiful room of all. He finally chose the grand salon, where the walls were covered with tapestries and wood carvings. He lit the numerous candelabra, put his knapsack in the corner, and hung up his sword on a nail. Then he settled down at a table on which he put his magic bag. In a little while, Fedor took out his tobacco pouch, filled his pipe, and calmly began to smoke.

But when the twelve strokes of midnight sounded from the church nearby, a crowd of demons appeared and began to swarm through the palace. They filled the rooms with dreadful sounds of screams, evil laughter, blows, and wild pursuits.

"Ah, it is you, soldier, who are here!" they shouted, making horrible faces.

"Yes, it is I, Fedor!" calmly announced the courageous visitor. "I have come to spend a night with you, for I wanted to see this palace."

"Then," said the devils, grinding their teeth, "then you will have to play cards with us. It is the tradition. We have not played with a good soldier like you for a long time!"

"Gladly," said Fedor. "I just happen to have a deck of cards in my bag. Here it is."

Saying this, he took out his cards and immediately began to deal. They played the first game, and the soldier won. They played the second game, and the soldier won again. The devils were as determined as they were dishonest. But they cheated and played their tricks in vain—the soldier won again and again!

Before daybreak they were obliged to place all the silver that the soldier had won on the table, and Fedor quickly swept it up.

"Wait, soldier!" the devils cried. "There is still a little of the night left before daybreak. We have in our treasure chests fifty crowns of gold and as many crowns of silver. We are going to play for them, and this time we will beat you!"

Whereupon a horrible little devil brought the pieces of gold and silver and piled them on the table. As they played, the devils ground their teeth, squinted their eyes, and clenched their crooked hands. As for brave soldier Fedor, he continued to play tirelessly for he still felt very fresh and very strong.

And again, to the great fury of all the demons, the beautiful piles of gold and silver coins began to melt like snow in the sun into the soldier's pockets and knapsack, filling them to overflowing!

Then, as dawn approached, all the devils started to insult the soldier and clamor at him

> By our chief, Satan!
> By death and blood!
> By fire and hell!
> Let us kill this thief so bold,
> and take back our silver and gold!

But soldier Fedor was as calm as he had always been in battle. And he did not waste a moment! He opened his magic bag wide and recited

> Hop quick! Hop quack!
> May all the devils
> go into my sack!

Hardly had he finished saying these words, when the devils,

one after another, disappeared into the bag. There were so very many that they were piled on top of one another and could barely breathe, and nothing more was heard from them.

Fedor slept peacefully until noon, and the king, who had not forgotten the mad undertaking of the brave soldier, was worried because he had not seen him again. He sent some of his men to the palace to find out what had happened to him.

"If he is dead," the king said, "remove his body from the palace with respect. He was a courageous soldier."

But when the men arrived at the palace, soldier Fedor, with a very satisfied look, was walking through the vast halls smoking his pipe!

"Hello, brave soldier!" cried the envoys of the king, who had hardly dared to enter the haunted palace. "We really expected to find you dead, and we came to get your body. By all the czars of great Russia! How did you spend the night, and how did you last until morning? Did you see any devils?"

"Why talk about devils? Look, rather, at how much gold and silver I have here!" answered soldier Fedor, laughing.

The king's men could not believe their eyes! They were so astonished that they wanted to ride back immediately to tell their amazing story to the king. Besides, they were still afraid of the devils!

"Wait, good people! All the devils and demons of hell are the same if you do not see them! I will take care of them. You go on, and send back to me two blacksmiths with their anvil and hammers as soon as possible."

The king's men did not understand what this was all about, but they were so happy to be able to leave the haunted palace, that they rushed out and rode off to tell the blacksmiths. The blacksmiths, hearing talk of gold and silver, left immediately and soon arrived at the palace, laden with an anvil and heavy hammers.

"Let's go!" ordered soldier Fedor. "Take that sack off the wall, put it on the anvil, and beat it as hard as if you were striking iron!"

The blacksmiths took the bag off the wall and felt that it was extraordinarily heavy. They were afraid that it might be filled with the gold and silver of which they had heard the king's men speak

"It is neither gold nor silver," Fedor assured them. "It is the DEVIL!"

"Exactly! Exactly! I am the devil!" cried each one of the demons piled up inside the bag.

Then the blacksmiths set up their anvil, put the sack on it, and went to it—BANG! BANG! They started to beat it. The heavy blows fell on the magic bag as if they were striking iron.

The cries of the devils echoed through the palace, "Ouch! Oh! Ayeee! Whee! Brave soldier! Brave Fedor! Stop having us beaten! Have pity on us! Spare us! Open your sack and give us our liberty. We will never again do any harm in this palace! Not one of us will ever again cross this threshold! Let the king move in. We will flee one hundred leagues away and we will never again return!"

The soldier finally told the blacksmiths to put down their hammers. And as soon as he opened his sack, all the devils burst out in one spurt and disappeared without saying another word.

Only one little lame devil, less speedy than the others, did not escape. Soldier Fedor kept this one carefully closed up in his bag and almost forgot about him.

As soon as the king was informed of the outcome of Fedor's amazing adventure, he called the soldier to him to congratulate and reward him. From that moment on Fedor had a very easy life and a profusion of wealth. The king was his friend and the entire court honored him. The broken windowpanes were replaced, everything the demons had destroyed was repaired, and the king finally moved into his palace.

Soldier Fedor became the king's steward. In all circumstances he always knew how to act bravely and intelligently. Soon Fedor married a beautiful young girl of the court, the

charming Helena, and they had a son whom they named Vassili.

Alas, the child fell gravely ill when he was seven years old. All the doctors were puzzled. They did not know what to make of his mysterious illness, and all their treatments were in vain.

Then Fedor remembered the little lame devil in the bottom of his sack. He had been so happy that he had forgotten all about it until this moment, but he quickly found his magic bag.

"Tell me, lame devil, are you still there? I have need of you."

"How can I be of service, steward Fedor?"

"My son, Vassili, is sick. He is going to die! The doctors cannot do anything to cure his illness; but you, lame devil, do you not possess the secret that could cure him?"

"Yes, I do possess it. But first let me out of here!"

"But what if you are tricking me? After all, you are only a devil!"

The little devil swore by Lucifer and on all the horns of all the devils in hell that he never had such an idea. Then Fedor untied the bag and the lame devil slipped out. The little devil immediately took from his pocket a glass which he filled with very pure spring water. He placed the glass at Vassili's bedside and told Fedor to look long and hard at the water in the glass.

For a long time Fedor stared through the glass at the clear spring water.

"Well? What do you see?" asked the little devil impatiently.

"I see the face of Death near my son," Fedor answered sadly.

"And where, exactly, is Death?"

"At my son's feet."

"Then your son will live," said the lame devil. "Take the glass and throw several drops of water on the sick boy, and the evil spell—for that is what has caused his illness—will leave him at once."

Fedor sprinkled his son with the clear water, and in a moment the illness left him and he regained his strength!

"Thank you, good little devil!" cried Fedor gratefully. "I give you your freedom, but I will keep your magic glass!"

However the little lame devil had already disappeared!

Fedor took up again his happy life with his wife, Helena, whom he loved very much, and his son, Vassili, who was now healthy and strong. Fedor lived with his family in part of the palace and faithfully performed his duties as the king's steward.

Often people came to consult him about illness, for the affair of the magic glass soon became known throughout the kingdom. Fedor was a good man. He liked to help people, and he would gladly go to the bedside of those who were ill, be they simple peasants or important dignitaries of the kingdom. Thanks to his magic glass, he had often been able to chase Death away, and his reputation kept growing.

One day the king himself fell ill. All the greatest doctors of the land were immediately called to his bedside. But they did not know what remedies to give the king, and each day he became weaker and weaker.

The king sent for his steward, who filled his magic glass with spring water and put it near the bed. Fedor gazed into the glass, and through the clear water he saw DEATH! But Death was so close to the king's head, that Fedor knew his poor master had only a few more hours to live.

"Tell me what you see, steward Fedor," the king barely had the strength to say.

Your Majesty," sadly replied Fedor, "no one can save you. Already I see Death carrying you away!"

"'You who have so often driven Death away, you who have cured so many sick people, can you not do anything for me, your king?"

Fedor started to think as hard as he could, seeking with all his might for something he could still do for his king. Then he started to conjure up Death, speaking to it thus—"Death! Let my king live! Take me in his place. Of course, I'm not a king; but for you, one dead man is as good as another!"

And again Fedor looked through the glass filled with clear water. Then he saw Death change its place from the head to the feet of the king. At that moment Fedor sprinkled the sick king as the little lame devil had taught him to do. Immediately the king arose. He was completly cured!

Steward Fedor spoke again to Death, "Death, grant me a delay of only a few minutes to go home to warn my wife and my son and give them my last wishes."

"Go ahead," agreed Death. "But I will be following you!"

Hardly had Fedor arrived home, when he became gravely ill. Death was at his bedside.

"Say your farewells quickly, Fedor!" Death said to him. "You have only three more minutes to see the light of day!"

Then, in a last effort, Fedor stretched out his hand and grabbed his magic bag, which was hanging at the head of his bed. He had just enough strength left to open it very wide and say to Death, "It's between the two of us now, for I am not dead yet!" And then he quickly recited

> Hop quick! Hop quack!
> You must enter
> into this sack!

At that very instant, Death was in the magic bag!

The king's steward, immediately cured, jumped out of bed and kissed his wife and son. After carefully buckling his magic sack, he threw it over his shoulder as though it were an ordinary piece of baggage, and started off toward the forest of Briansk.

When he came to the thickest part of the forest, he chose a very high tree and climbed up to the top. There he took the bag from his shoulder and hung it from the very highest branch of the tree. That done, he went home, well satisfied

with what he had just accomplished and very glad to still be alive!

From then on, no one died in that country, because Death was tightly shut up in the sack and the sack was hanging deep in the forest. And, of course, Fedor had no intention of ever looking for it again.

Many happy years passed for steward Fedor and his family, and for the king and his. And in all those years no one died. There were only births in this country!

But one day steward Fedor met on the road a very, very old woman — so old that she was bent completely to the ground — so old that she shook at the least breath of air like the flame of a candle about to go out!

"Little grandmother! How can you still be here when you are so old?" Fedor asked her.

"Alas, Fedor, it is your fault! The moment I was about to die, you went and closed Death up in your sack and hid it in the woods. Believe me, I would be very happy to be at rest. You had no right to close Death up in your bag, steward Fedor! Man is made to live and then to die. Great is your fault!"

And the old woman, tottering and bent, continued on her way while Fedor thought over what she had said.

"That old woman is right," he said to himself. "It is time for me to go and free Death. It's all right with me if Death takes me now, for my life has been full. I have some sins on my conscience, but I have done a lot of good also."

And courageously, thinking all the while of his wife and son, whom he loved tenderly, Fedor set out for the forest of Briansk.

When he came to the thickest part of the forest, he approached the tall tree and raised his eyes. Sure enough, way at the top his sack still hung, swinging to and fro although there wasn't the slightest breath of wind!

"Hey there, Death, are you still up there?" cried Fedor.

And the voice of Death came down to him. "I am!" answered Death, simply.

Then steward Fedor climbed the tree and took down his sack. He opened it at once and pleaded with Death to finish him off as quickly as possible.

But Death fled with such speed that Fedor did not even have time to catch a glimpse of him! And so he climbed down from the tree, crossed the forest of Briansk in the other direction, and returned home, happy to still be alive.

"My word!" he said to himself, "Death must have something more important to do than to kill me now! It will come back for me in its own good time."

Indeed, steward Fedor lived happily for a very, very long time, almost as if life need never end!

Maria Marina, Czar Nicolas, and the Giant Vatsek

Prince Nicolas had three young sisters—Tania, Olga, and Anna—three pretty little princesses ready for marriage, whom his father, Czar Ivan, had entrusted to his son's care as he was dying. Nicolas was to marry them off to princes who would come to ask for their hands in marriage, on one condition—each of the princesses must love her prince!

One summer day Prince Nicolas was playing croquet with his sisters in front of the palace greenhouse, when suddenly the sky became dark and it started to pour.

"Let's get inside quickly, little sisters!" cried Nicolas.

The Prince and the three princesses ran to take shelter in the greenhouse. But at that instant, a terrible clap of thunder shook the entire countryside. The roof of the greenhouse opened, and a falcon whose wings were trembling entered through the ceiling and came to perch at Nicolas's feet. Before the astonished eyes of the prince and the three princesses, he immediately transformed himself into a very handsome young man!

"I greet you, Prince Nicolas," he said, bowing. "I greet you, lovely princesses! Pardon me for having interrupted your game."

"May we know who you are?" asked Nicolas.

"I am Prince Falcon, come from my kingdom of the steppes to meet you, Prince Nicolas, for I wish to ask for the hand of your sister Tania."

"I am very flattered," answered Nicolas, "but first I would like to know what my sister Tania thinks of you."

"I love Prince Falcon," Princess Tania answered her brother. "He will bring me happiness and I will make him happy!"

A great celebration was arranged, and the very next day Princess Tania married Prince Falcon who took her to his kingdom of the steppes.

A year passed. Prince Nicolas watched over princesses Olga and Anna. One summer day, while he was walking with them in the gardens of the palace, an enormous gust of wind surprised them.

"Let's go in quickly before the storm comes, little sisters!" cried Nicolas. But hardly had they returned to the palace, when they heard a terrible clap of thunder. The roof of the palace opened and an eagle with an extraordinary wingspread entered through the ceiling. He perched at Prince Nicolas's feet and immediately transformed himself into a wonderful young man right in front of the astonished eyes of Prince Nicolas and the princesses!

"I greet you, Prince Nicolas," he said, bowing. "I greet you lovely princesses. Pardon me for having interrupted your walk."

"May we know who you are?" asked Prince Nicolas.

"I am Prince Eagle, come from my kingdom of the mountains to ask for the hand of Princess Olga."

"I am very happy about that," said Nicolas, "but let the princess herself tell us if she wishes to take you as her husband."

"I love Prince Eagle," answered Princess Olga. "He will bring me happiness and I will make him happy!"

A great celebration was arranged, and the very next day Princess Olga married Prince Eagle who took her to his kingdom of the mountains.

Another year passed. Prince Nicolas watched over his youngest sister, Princess Anna. One summer day, while he was picking fruit with her in the orchards of the palace, the sky suddenly became dark and great gusts of wind blew up.

"Let us run for shelter quickly, little sister!" cried Prince Nicolas.

And they went running home to the palace. But hardly had they reached shelter, when an enormous clap of thunder shook the whole palace. The roof opened and a black crow with splendid plumage entered through the ceiling. He came to perch at Nicolas's feet, and before the astonished eyes of Prince Nicolas and little Princess Anna, he changed himself into a magnificent young man!

"I greet you, Prince Nicolas!" he said, bowing. "I greet you, beautiful Princess Anna! Pardon me for having interrupted your fruit gathering."

"May we know who you are?" asked Prince Nicolas.

"I am Prince Crow, come from my kingdom of the forests to ask for Princess Anna's hand in marriage."

"I am delighted," answered Nicolas, "but let the princess herself tell us if she wishes to take you for her husband."

"I love Prince Crow," affirmed Princess Anna. "He will bring me happiness and I will make him happy."

A great celebration was arranged, and the very next day Princess Anna married Prince Crow who took her to his kingdom of the forests.

Prince Nicolas remained alone. Another year passed, and Nicolas was crowned czar. In spite of the responsibilities of his

kingdom, he began to be troubled about his three sisters and decided to undertake a long journey to visit them. He would visit Prince Falcon and Princess Tania in the kingdom of the steppes, Prince Eagle and Princess Olga in the kingdom of the mountains, and Prince Crow and Princess Anna in the kingdom of the forests.

After entrusting his subjects, his lands, and all his possessions to a council of wise lords, Czar Nicolas left alone on his horse, Droujok, and traveled for three months.

Finally one evening he found himself at the bottom of the high, thick walls of an immense castle. An entire army was encamped there, ready to march. It was not the castle of Prince Falcon, nor the castle of Prince Eagle, nor the castle of Prince Crow. Nicolas wished to know to whom the army and the castle belonged.

"Whom do all these soldiers obey?" he asked the first soldier that he met.

"We are all under the orders of the young czarina, Maria Marina, who has declared war on the enemies of our kingdom," answered the officer. "Our troops will soon be ready."

"I am a friend," declared Czar Nicolas, curious to meet this warrior czarina. "May I meet your chief?"

Thus it was that Czar Nicolas, forgetting for a moment the purpose of his trip, was brought to the tent of the warrior czarina, Maria Marina, who was to change his entire destiny.

Czarina Maria Marina came up to him to welcome him and the czar thought that she was by far the most beautiful young girl he had ever seen. He wondered how she could possibly have enemies to fight against! The czarina gave him a room in her castle that very evening and begged him to stay as long as he desired.

Two days passed and Czar Nicolas could not wait any longer to declare his love to the czarina.

"Maria Marina," he said to her, "you are the most beautiful

little czarina in all of great Russia! I wish to marry you and take you to my kingdom!"

"Prince Nicolas," she answered him, "I do want to marry you and follow you to your kingdom for I love you, too. But I have promised my subjects to defend them against our enemies. My army is ready for battle and I must lead it. Let us be married, but permit me to leave tomorrow. I promise to return as soon as we have been victorious."

That very day Czar Nicolas married the warrior czarina, and she finished the last preparations for battle.

On the following day, Maria Marina entrusted her castle and her kingdom to Czar Nicolas, saying to him, "Dear Nicolas, here are all the keys to my castle. You will be able to enter wherever you wish, from the storerooms to the lofts, from the cellars to the attics. But you must absolutely never go up to the top of the highest tower which looks over all the roofs of my castle! At the top of that tower there is a room. This room is closed by a door with seven locks for which I give you seven keys. But do not ever try to get in there!"

And Maria Marina, the beautiful little czarina, sped off on her horse at the head of her army, to the sound of trumpets and bells.

Alone, Czar Nicolas soon began to be bored. He missed his wife very much, and the desire to visit his three sisters was always in his heart. If he had not promised Maria Marina to watch over the affairs of her kingdom, he would have started at once on a journey to see his sisters.

Three weeks had passed since the czarina had left at the head of her army, and Nicolas had not received any news from her. One day, while he was sadly walking in the courtyard of the castle, the very highest tower attracted his attention and for the first time his curiosity was stirred.

By now he was familiar with the entire castle, but never had he gone up to that tower. What precious thing was closed up behind a door with seven locks? Nicolas burned with the desire to know. It suddenly seemed to him that in the absence

of Maria Marina, only one thing mattered to him—to discover what there was in that tower. And he had the seven keys that would open the seven locks!

He rushed up the stairways of the castle, then climbed the tower stairs without even stopping to catch his breath. Soon he was in front of the door with seven locks.

The keys turned effortlessly in the well-oiled locks and the door opened wide. An enormous giant was lying on the floor, held down by twelve chains!

"Czar Nicolas! Czar Nicolas! Have pity on me! Give me something to drink!" pleaded the giant in an astonishingly weak voice for a being of such size.

The czar could not refuse. He went into the courtyard, filled a pail with water, and took it back up into the tower. He gave it to the giant, who emptied it with one swallow.

The giant's voice was a little stronger when he pleaded again, "Czar Nicolas! Czar Nicolas! Give me more water to drink. That was not enough!"

And the czar went down once again into the courtyard and came back to the giant with a pail full of water. The giant emptied it as he had the first one and asked again for more, "Czar Nicolas! Czar Nicolas! Give me something to drink once more!"

But after drinking for the third time, he regained all his strength. In a single movement he broke all his chains and stood up. At that very moment the bells rang and the trumpets sounded to announce the victorious return of the little warrior queen.

The giant came out of his prison and exclaimed, "Thank you, Czar Nicolas! You have given me back my strength, but you have lost Maria Marina. For I am the giant Vatsek and I want Maria Marina for myself!"

From the top of the tower, he jumped into space, snatched the little czarina from her saddle, and disappeared with her beyond the mountains.

Leaving the government of the kingdom to a council of lords, Czar Nicolas mounted his horse, Droujok, and galloped off in pursuit of the giant. He would bring back Maria Marina no matter what might happen!

But he galloped for three days and three nights without finding a trace of the giant. On the morning of the fourth day he came to the gates of a magnificent castle. Perched high on an oak tree, a falcon with trembling wings guarded the entrance. As soon as he saw Czar Nicolas, he flew down and immediately transformed himself into a handsome young man whom the czar recognized with joy.

"Princess Tania! Princess Tania! Our brother is here!" called out Prince Falcon.

And Princess Tania ran up and kissed her brother tenderly, asking him to stay for a long time in the kingdom of the steppes. But Czar Nicolas would stay only one day and one night with Prince Falcon and Princess Tania.

"I must leave in search of my wife, the beautiful Czarina Maria Marina," he said to them. "Because of my mistake, the giant Vatsek seized her and carried her off far from her kingdom and far from me!"

"Leave, if you believe that it is your duty," Prince Falcon answered, "but know that you will have trouble conquering the giant Vatsek and that you will face many dangers! Leave us your silver spoon, Prince Nicolas. We will think of you when we look at it, and we will know if you need us."

So the czar left his silver spoon at Prince Falcon's castle, tenderly kissed his sister Tania, and courageously took up his pursuit.

He galloped for another three days and three nights without finding a trace of the giant. On the morning of the fourth day, he came to the gates of a magnificent castle. Perched high on an oak tree, a powerful eagle guarded the entrance. As soon as he saw Czar Nicolas, he flew down and immediately transformed himself into a handsome young man whom the czar recognized with joy.

"Princess Olga! Princess Olga! Our brother is here!" called out Prince Eagle.

And Princess Olga ran up to her brother and kissed him tenderly, asking him to stay for a long time in the kingdom of the mountains. But Czar Nicolas would stay only one day and one night with Prince Eagle and Princess Olga.

"I must leave in search of my wife, the beautiful Czarina Maria Marina," he said to them. "Because of my mistake, the giant Vatsek seized her and carried her off far from her kingdom and far from me!"

"Leave, if you believe that it is your duty," Prince Eagle answered, "but know that you will have trouble conquering the giant Vatsek and that you will face many dangers! Leave us your silver fork, Prince Nicolas. We will think of you when we look at it, and we will know if you need us."

So the czar left his silver fork at Prince Eagle's castle, tenderly kissed his sister Olga, and courageously took up his pursuit.

Again he galloped for three days and three nights without finding any sign of the giant. On the morning of the fourth day, he came to the gates of a castle even more beautiful than the first two. Perched high on an oak tree, a crow with wings as black as night seemed to be waiting for him. As soon as he saw Czar Nicolas, he flew down and immediately transformed himself into a handsome young man whom the czar recognized with joy.

"Princess Anna! Princess Anna!" exclaimed Prince Crow. "Our brother is here!"

And Princess Anna came running, kissed her brother tenderly, and asked him to stay for a long time in the kingdom of the forests.

But Czar Nicolas refused once again and would stay but one single day and one single night with Prince Crow and Princess Anna.

"I must leave in search of my wife, the beautiful Czarina Maria Marina," he said to them. "Because of my mistake, the

46

giant Vatsek seized her and carried her off far from her kingdom and far from me!"

"Leave, if you believe it is your duty," Prince Crow answered him, "but know that you will have trouble conquering the giant Vatsek and that you will face many dangers. Leave us your silver knife, Prince Nicolas. We will think of you when we look at it, and we will know if you need us."

So the czar left his silver knife at Prince Crow's castle, tenderly kissed his sister Anna, and courageously took up his pursuit of the giant Vatsek.

The next evening he came to an absolutely enormous castle and learned that it belonged to the giant Vatsek. He encountered neither guards nor servants, but was happy to find his darling Maria Marina, who cried for joy as she kissed him.

"Oh Nicolas," she said to him. "Why did you open the door to the giant? If you had not given him a drink of water, his power would have disappeared forever!"

"Forgive me, Maria Marina, and let us escape now before the giant Vatsek returns."

"You are strong, Nicolas, but the power of the giant Vatsek is greater than we are," sighed the little czarina.

"But my love for you, Maria Marina, is greater than the giant's!" And Czar Nicolas lifted Maria Marina onto his horse, and starting off at a gallop, soon disappeared into the woods.

At nightfall the giant Vatsek returned from hunting. In front of the entrance to the castle his fantastic horse started to kick and paw the ground in fury.

"Why are you angry?" the giant asked him, as if he expected a response.

And the extraordinary horse did indeed answer in a human voice, "Giant! Czar Nicolas came and carried off Czarina Maria Marina while we were hunting!"

"How much time do we need to catch up with them?" asked the giant, who wished first to take time to drink, eat, rest, and sleep.

"Only a few minutes," answered his horse. "Even if we

leave tomorrow morning, we will easily catch up with them!"

So the next morning, the giant Vatsek, mounted on his horse, which was fleet as the wind, caught up with Czar Nicolas and took Maria Marina away from him.

"I spare you your life, Czar Nicolas, because you saved mine by giving me some water to drink," the giant, who was already far away, exclaimed, "but do not forget that the giant Vatsek is powerful and cruel!"

Czar Nicolas, left alone in the middle of the road with his tired horse, wept with discouragement and sorrow. But his love for Maria Marina was greater than his despair. He mounted his horse, turned around, and rode back to the castle of the giant.

As before, he met neither guards nor servants, and again he picked up Maria Marina, lifted her to his horse's back, and carried her off at a gallop.

At nightfall the giant Vatsek returned from hunting, and again was astounded to feel his horse rear up and paw the ground with fury at the entrance to the castle.

"What's the matter with you now, horse? Why are you angry?" asked the giant, convinced that Maria Marina was waiting for him and that Czar Nicolas would not dare defy him a second time.

"Czar Nicolas came to take back Maria Marina!" answered the horse.

"Can we catch them?" asked the exasperated giant.

"Even if you took the time to sow some wheat, harvest it, grind it, make flour with it, knead some bread, bake it in the oven, and eat it, we would be sure of overtaking them in a few bounds, for, as you well know, I am a most extraordinary horse!"

"I will not wait that long!" shouted Vatsek. "I want Maria Marina in my castle this very evening!"

And in two bounds they overtook the fleeing couple.

"Czar Nicolas! Once again I spare your life, for thanks to you, I have regained my strength!" the giant cried out to him

as he snatched up Maria Marina, "but the third time you will die!"

Left alone in the middle of the road, Czar Nicolas wept again. But his love for Maria Marina was stronger than his despair, stronger even than his fear of death. Once again he went back to the castle of the giant Vatsek where Maria Marina was grieving.

"Escape without me," she said to him, "for this time the giant will kill you."

"I prefer to die rather than to live without you," Czar Nicolas answered. And again he carried off the little czarina at a gallop.

Returning at nightfall, the giant was astounded to feel his horse kick and paw the ground in fury when he came to the entrance of the castle.

"Could it be possible that Czar Nicolas has once again carried off Maria Marina?" he asked his horse.

"He came back one more time!"

"And this will be the last one, for he is going to die!" shouted the giant.

And in two bounds, horse and rider caught up with the fleeing couple! The giant Vatsek seized Czar Nicolas, shut him up in a barrel, and threw the barrel into the sea! Then he returned to his castle, carrying Maria Marina on his extraordinary horse.

At that very moment the silver spoon, fork, and knife that Czar Nicolas had left with his sisters became completely black!

"Our brother is in danger!"

"Our brother is going to die!"

"We must save our brother!"

And each princess called her husband.

Immediately Prince Eagle flew out over the ocean and located the barrel. Prince Falcon dragged it to the shore. Prince Crow flew to find some brandy. The three bird princes broke open the barrel and found the czar who seemed to be dead. Fortunately, they were able to revive him by giving him some brandy to drink.

"Ah, I have slept well," sighed Czar Nicolas as he stretched.

"Without us you would have slept for eternity!" answered his three brothers-in-law. "Can't you stay now for a while with one of us?"

"I must return without delay to the giant's castle, for I must rescue Maria Marina whom I love!" cried Czar Nicolas, ready to leave again.

"But the giant has an incredible horse!" exclaimed Prince Falcon.

"A horse as swift as the wind!" added Prince Eagle.

"As fast as you can flee, he will always catch you!" said Prince Crow.

"Listen to our advice, Czar Nicolas," said the three princes together. "If you do not, you will never be able to conquer the giant and you will die—go to the giant's castle and find Maria Marina again, but you must not try to take her away. Only try to learn from her how the giant got his extraordinary horse."

So Czar Nicolas set out again on his journey and soon reached the giant's castle. The little czarina, who had thought him to be dead, cried with joy on seeing him. Czar Nicolas said to her, "This evening when the giant returns from hunting, try to find out where his marvelous horse that runs like the wind came from. Listen well to his answer and repeat his words to me exactly."

That very evening the little czarina questioned the giant, "Tell me, giant, where does your extraordinary horse that runs like the wind come from?"

The giant Vatsek was very proud of his horse and did not hesitate to answer her, "Learn, pretty little czarina, that at the end of great Russia, beyond the kingdom of the greatest czar, and across a river of fire, there is a huge prairie. On that prairie lives a cruel sorceress who raises the fastest horses in the world! I took care of her horses for three days, in return for which she gave me one of her colts."

"And how did you manage to cross the river of fire?"

"I have a magic handkerchief in my left pocket. You just have to shake it three times to the right and say

Strabridge! Strafire!
Rise up bridge
over the fire!

in order that a bridge be immediately raised over the river of fire. When you shake the handkerchief three times to the left and say

Strabridge! Strafire!
Disappear bridge
over the fire!

the bridge completely disappears!"

Maria Marina listened very hard and memorized the magic words perfectly. And she also remembered where Nicolas should go to find the sorceress who raised the fastest horses in the world.

As soon as the giant was asleep, she took the magic handkerchief from his left pocket and quickly went to join Nicolas, who was waiting for her at the gates of the castle. Maria Marina gave him the handkerchief and repeated to him exactly what she had just learned.

Czar Nicolas memorized the magic words, put the handkerchief in the bottom of his pocket, kissed Maria Marina, and immediately left for the land of the sorceress.

He walked for days and days and weeks and weeks without stopping, for he had to go to the end of great Russia, and he knew that his Maria Marina was waiting for him in the castle of the giant Vatsek.

One evening, tired and hungry, he met a blackbird surrounded by her little ones.

"I would gladly catch these birds and cook them," he said aloud to himself.

With that the blackbird started to speak to him, "Do not eat me, Czar Nicolas, and do not eat my little ones. One day we will be of service to you!"

So Czar Nicolas was content with some wild berries, and he continued on his way. But he was still very hungry when a little while later he met a lioness and her cub.

He could not help but say aloud, "I did not cook the birds, but perhaps I will be able to eat a little lion."

Thereupon the lioness said to him, "Keep your hunger to yourself, Czar Nicolas! Do not touch my little lion! The moment will come when I will be able to be of service to you!"

So the czar went on walking without touching the young lion. A little farther on, he noticed a swarm of bees in a tree.

"I was not able to eat the birds or the little lion," he said aloud, "at least I am going to be able to satisfy my hunger with honey!"

But the queen of the bees immediately began to speak to him, "Do not touch my beehive, Czar Nicolas! Do not eat my honey! The moment will come when I will be able to be of service to you!"

So the czar left the honey and went on walking. To bolster up his courage, he thought of his beautiful Czarina Maria Marina, still a prisoner of the terrible giant.

Finally one morning he came to the bank of the river of fire, which it was necessary for him to cross in order to reach the land of the sorceress. There he took the magic handkerchief out of his pocket, shook it three times to the right, and repeated as he had been told

Strabridge! Strafire!
Rise up bridge
over the fire!

Immediately the arch of a silver bridge rose above the flames and the czar, astonished at his power, crossed safely over the river of fire. He remembered to make the bridge disappear, and then he went straight to the sorceress who was just leaving her house.

"Good day, little grandmother," he said to her joyously.

But the sorceress looked at him with ugly eyes, and said severely, "Why did you come here, Czar Nicolas, and what do you want?"

"I want you to give me a horse as swift as the wind," answered Nicolas.

"All my horses are as swift as the wind," answered the sorceress dryly, "but I do not give them! One must earn them!"

"And how may I earn one, then?" asked Nicolas.

"Remain in my service for three days, lead my horses to pasture, and bring them back to the stable for me every night. If I am missing one, I will throw you into the river of fire," hissed the evil sorceress.

Czar Nicolas, who had crossed all of great Russia to bring back one of the famous horses, accepted the proposition at once.

The sorceress gave him something to eat and drink and ordered him to take all her horses out of the paddock immediately and lead them to the huge prairie. And that is what Nicolas did.

But hardly had he opened the gates of the paddock, when all the horses raced out at a great gallop, scattered in the immense fields of the prairie, and disappeared without a trace!

All day long the czar looked for the horses and called to them in vain. Desperate and exhausted, he sat down at last on the grass, and in no time he fell fast asleep.

The sun was about to set when he awakened to hear the voice of a blackbird saying in his ear, "Wake up, Czar Nicolas, and rejoice! Thanks to us, all the horses are back in the stable!"

The czar got up and ran to the stable. There he heard the awful voice of the sorceress reproaching the horses for having returned. He also heard the horses answer her.

"Hundreds of birds came from all sides and pecked at us with their sharp beaks to force us to return. We did indeed have to return to the stable!"

"Tomorrow," the sorceress said to them, "instead of disappearing into the prairie, you are going to hide in the deepest woods. And you are absolutely not to return to the stable!"

The czar slept peacefully the whole night through. At sunrise the sorceress called him and said, "Lead the horses to pasture as you did yesterday. But be careful not to lose a single one. If you do, I will throw you into the river of fire!"

But hardly had Nicolas opened the gates of the paddock, when all the horses raced out at a great gallop, scattered in all directions, and hid in the deepest woods. All day long the czar searched for them and called to them in vain.

When the sun was just about to set, a lioness arrived, followed by her cub, and said to Nicolas, "Czar Nicolas, rejoice! All the horses are back in the stable!"

The czar ran back to the stable in time to hear the ugly voice of the sorceress asking her horses, "Why did you all return and why did you not listen to me, cursed horses?"

"We did go to the woods," answered the horses, "but some lions surrounded us and pushed us towards the stable. What else could we do?"

"Tomorrow," the sorceress said to them, "instead of going to the woods, you must go towards the beach, hide in the deepest part of the ocean, and above all do not return to the stable!"

The following morning Nicolas went again to lead the horses to the wide fields of the prairie, but once more they immediately escaped and galloped towards the beach. The czar tried to follow them, but he soon lost all hope of ever seeing them again for all of them, one after the other, disappeared into the hollows of the waves!

He waited for them until sunset, calling them in vain, and despaired. But along came a bee to whisper in his ear, "Czar Nicolas, the horses are safe! Thanks to us, you have won! But whatever you do, do not wait for the wicked sorceress to keep her promise. When she falls asleep, choose a horse and flee with it towards the river of fire!"

Nicolas ran towards the stable and heard the sorceress shouting at her horses, "Why did you return, cursed horses?"

And the horses answered her, "A swarm of bees buzzed around us! They forced us to return by stinging us until we bled!"

The furious sorceress went to bed fuming. She fell asleep searching in her wicked head for a new test she could set Nicolas the next day so that she could plunge him into the river of fire.

But Nicolas did not waste a minute! As soon as he heard the sorceress snoring, he chose her most beautiful horse, jumped on its back, and galloped off to the river of fire. There he stopped, took the magic handkerchief out of his pocket, and waved it three times to the right, saying

> Strabridge! Strafire!
> Raise up bridge
> over the fire!

Immediately the arch of a silver bridge was raised over the flames. Czar Nicolas crossed it swiftly, and once on the other side, he shook the magic handkerchief three times to the left, saying

> Strabridge! Strafire!
> Disappear bridge
> over the fire!

Then he left at a gallop without looking back, and his wonderful horse ran like the wind! But just at that moment the sorceress woke up and realized that Nicolas was gone.

At once she mounted one of her horses and rushed off in pursuit of him. In her haste and anger she did not notice that the magic bridge was quickly fading away. There was just a little bridge as fragile as an arch of crystal still rising above the flames. Nevertheless she ventured onto it and the arch gave way under her weight. The sorceress and all her wickedness disappeared into the flames!

Meanwhile Nicolas on his fantastically fleet horse had already reached the castle of the giant Vatsek, where his wife, the little czarina, was waiting for him.

"Quick, Maria Marina!" he cried, without even taking the time to kiss her. "Jump on behind me and let us flee! My horse will take us away as quickly as the wind and the giant Vatsek will never be able to catch up!"

And in an instant the two arrived at the castle of Prince Crow in the kingdom of the forests, where Princess Anna welcomed them joyfully.

At nightfall, when the giant Vatsek, coming back from hunting, arrived at the gates of his castle, he was astounded to feel his horse rear up and paw the ground in fury.

"What is the matter, horse?" he asked him nervously. "Has some misfortune occurred?"

"Czar Nicolas came again! He has carried off Maria Marina!" answered the horse.

"Can we overtake them?" asked the giant.

"No, giant, this time we cannot," anwered the horse. "Czar Nicolas has found a horse even faster than I. He has already arrived at the castle of Prince Crow in the kingdom of the woods. We can no longer do anything to defeat him, and the little czarina is lost to you!"

The giant was furious and he stalked into his castle never to come out again, so great was his anger at having been beaten!

Czar Nicolas and Maria Marina stayed for some time with Prince Crow and Princess Anna. Then they stayed with

Prince Eagle and Princess Olga for a while. And finally they visited Prince Falcon and Princess Tania.

They also stopped for a time in Maria Marina's kingdom, but at last they ended their long journey in Czar Nicolas's own kingdom, where a sumptuous feast awaited them. All the inhabitants of the city, dressed in their finest clothes, came out to welcome them, and each one drank to the health of Nicolas and Maria Marina.

In the evening, there was a grand ball by the light of torches. The czar and czarina danced all night and into the early hours of the morning and dazzled their guests with their beauty and grace.

Czar Nicolas and Czarina Maria Marina lived for a long time and were very happy together. And they never again heard from the giant Vatsek.

The String Bean That Went
Through
the Roof of the World

Not so very long ago, old Onuphre and his wife, old Euxenia, were still living in their little log cabin, for the good Lord did not want either of them in his heaven. And here is the reason why . . .

One day old Onuphre's rooster crowed, "Cock-a-doodle-doo! Cock-a-doodle-doo! I have found a string bean!"

The old man took the string bean and threw it under the table and forgot about it.

In her turn, old Euxenia's hen sang, "Cluck, cluck, cluck! I have found a lima bean! A lima bean!"

The old woman took the lima bean and threw it under the

table where it landed next to the string bean. Soon the lima bean and the string bean sprouted on the hard dirt floor and began to grow.

"What should we do?" asked the old woman. "Should we pull out the beans?"

"No," answered the old man. "We must cut the table apart so the beans can grow up." And old Onuphre sawed the table in half.

But the beans grew higher and higher. The vines were soon so tall that they almost touched the ceiling of the log cabin.

"What's to be done?" asked the old woman. "Must we pull out the string bean and the lima bean?"

"No," the old man answered again. "We must cut a hole in the roof." And the old man cut a hole in the roof of the cabin.

But the string bean and the lima bean grew taller and taller and stronger and stronger, so that they almost touched the sky.

"You see," said the old man, "I was right. The bean plants are arriving in heaven at this very moment!"

"Oh?" said the old woman, who didn't believe a word of it. "Let's go see for ourselves."

"If you wish," agreed the old man. "Let's try to climb up to heaven on the bean plants."

And so there they were, the two of them, climbing to heaven — the old man on the string bean plant and the old woman on the lima bean plant. Flabbergasted, the cock and the hen watched them climb to the sky.

"It's a hard climb!" sighed old Onuphre from time to time on his string bean plant.

"It's so high!" complained old Euxenia on her lima bean plant.

But just the same they managed to climb to the top of the string bean and lima bean plants. Then the old man and the old woman saw that they had indeed arrived in heaven.

"I see a little cabin all made of gold with a garden around it!" said the old woman.

"Let's go there," said the old man. "It must be the cabin of the good Lord!"

So old Onuphre and old Euxenia knocked on the door of the golden cabin.

"Enter!" cried the good Lord, who happened to be in. And they both went into the cabin.

"We are Onuphre and Euxenia," said the old woman. "We come from earth and we are very tired. Would you permit us to sleep in your cabin this evening?"

"You can sleep here this night," allowed the good Lord, "but you must not touch my little cakes!"

"We won't touch them," promised the old man and the old woman, who were dead tired.

But as soon as she got into bed, old Euxenia began to think of the little cakes. "How good they smell," she said very softly to the old man.

"Of course they do. They are the cakes of the good Lord," answered the old man.

"And how golden they are!" continued the old woman. "Ah, if only I could taste them."

"They are the cakes of the good Lord!" repeated the old man. "You know that you must not touch them. Isn't it enough to spend the night in his heaven?" said the old man as he fell asleep.

But the old woman could think only of the cakes. "Oh, those cakes! Those cakes! I must taste them! I will only take a little mouthful." And very quietly Euxenia got up and bit into a cake.

At once the cakes turned back into flour, butter, eggs and salt! The platter broke and the old man woke up!

All that night, old Euxenia tried to remake the little cakes and old Onuphre tried to put together the pieces of the platter. But try as they might, they could not succeed.

In the morning when the good Lord returned, the cakes immediately remade themselves and the pieces of the platter put themselves back together.

"You haven't touched my little cakes, have you?" asked the good Lord.

"Oh, no! Oh, no!" lied the two old people.

Then the good Lord was very sad, and at once Onuphre and Euxenia found themselves sliding down the string bean and lima bean plants. They soon arrived at their log cabin, where the rooster and the hen were waiting for them.

But the two old people could not forget their visit to heaven. They wanted to return and see again the good Lord in his golden cabin.

So the next morning they began to climb up the string bean and lima bean plants once more, and again they managed to reach heaven.

"Here we are again!" they said to the good Lord. "We are Onuphre and Euxenia and we are very old and very tired. We

will not ask you to let us sleep in your golden cabin, but would
you permit us to sleep outside your cabin this evening?"

"You may sleep in my vineyard," granted the good Lord,
"but whatever you do, do not touch my grapes!"

"We won't touch them," promised the two old people. And
they stretched out on the soft moss of the vineyard and fell
asleep.

But soon the old woman woke up and shook the old man.
"How good they smell, those bunches of grapes!" she said very
softly.

"Of course they do. They grow on the vines of the good
Lord," responded the old man.

"And how golden they are!" continued old Euxenia.

"They are the grapes of the good Lord! You know very well
that you must not touch them. Is it not wonderful enough to
be able to spend the night in his vineyard?" said the old man
as he fell asleep again.

But the old woman could think only of the beautiful clusters of grapes. "Oh those grapes! Those grapes! I must taste them! I will take only one grape."

And very quietly Euxenia got up and touched a grape. Immediately all the bunches of grapes fell from the vines of the good Lord and the old man woke up!

All that night old Euxenia and old Onuphre tried to fasten the bunches of grapes back onto the vines. But try as they might, they could not succeed.

In the morning when the good Lord returned, all the bunches of grapes fastened themselves back onto the vines.

"You haven't touched my grapes, have you?" asked the good Lord.

Oh, no! Oh, no!" the two old people lied again.

Then the good Lord became angry and chased them out of heaven.

Immediately they found themselves sliding down the string bean and lima bean plants, right to the bottom. There they were, back at their log cabin, where the rooster and the hen were waiting for them.

But Onuphre and Euxenia still could not forget heaven. They wanted to return and see the good Lord again. So the next morning they began once more to climb up the string bean and lima bean plants.

"Here we are again!" they said to the good Lord when they arrived. "Onuphre and Euxenia, even older and more tired. Would you permit us to sleep in heaven tonight?"

"Go into my carriage house," said the good Lord. "There is nothing to eat there, and you will be sheltered. But do not touch my carriages!"

"We will not touch them!" promised the two old people. And they stretched out on the straw in the carriage house and fell asleep.

Soon the old woman woke up and shook the old man. "I would certainly like to take a little carriage ride in heaven!" she said.

"These are the carriages of the good Lord! Remember, Euxenia, that we must not touch them!"

"I am only going to sit in this one," insisted the old woman very softly. "No one will ever know."

And that is what she did. Immediately the wheels of the carriage fell off and the carriage itself fell into pieces. The old man and the old woman spent the rest of the night trying to put it together again. But try as they might, they could not succeed.

In the morning when the good Lord returned, all the pieces of the carriage flew back into place.

"You haven't touched my carriage, have you?" asked the good Lord.

"Oh, no! Oh, no!" the old man and the old woman lied for the third time.

Then the good Lord flew into a great rage and threw them out of heaven at once!

"Hurry! Hurry!" said the old woman to the old man and the old man to the old woman, for they wished to escape the fury of the good Lord. And once again they were sliding down the string bean and lima bean plants as fast as they could.

But just before they got to the bottom, both bean plants broke! Then old Onuphre and old Euxenia fell head over heels into their garden, where the rooster and the hen were waiting for them.

The good Lord certainly did not want to see them in his heaven again for a very long time. And that is why old Onuphre and old Euxenia lived on in their little log cabin until they were very old indeed before the good Lord allowed them to return to paradise.

Axe Soup

Antoniev, the old cossack, had not had a horse for a long time. He was returning from the city on foot and he began to find the road very long. In addition, hunger was pinching at him! Not a ruble in his pocket, not even a piece of black bread or a cracker in his knapsack, and he still had several versts to go before arriving home.

He knocked at the door of a pretty little cabin at the entrance to a village, "Knock! Knock! Knock! Open your door to an old soldier who is returning from the city!" he called.

An old woman opened the door, happy to hear some fresh news from the city. But hardly had the old cossack seated himself near the stove, when he asked for something to eat.

"You wouldn't by chance have a good bowl of soup to give me, little grandmother, with a morsel of bread, and perhaps a piece of bacon? I have not eaten anything since this morning!"

"Alas, brave cossack, I am so poor that I, too, have not eaten since this morning. I have nothing to give you."

But old Antoniev, as exhausted and famished as he was, knew very well that he had not knocked at the door of a cottage so poor that there wasn't a bit of soup or bacon to give to a starving traveler.

"Well, if you have nothing, too bad!" he declared. "I will just rest here with you for a moment."

The old woman, who was not poor, but merely stingy, breathed a sigh of relief and sat down on the other side of the stove.

The old soldier had noticed an axe without a handle, lying forgotten under the table.

"Since you do not have anything to eat either, let us make some good soup with this axe, little grandmother."

The old woman raised her eyes heavenward, "What are you saying, cossack? Make soup from an axe?"

"Bring me a big pot. I am going to show you my recipe and then you can taste the soup," said the sly cossack. And he took the pot, filled it with water, and put it on the fire. Then he added the iron axe, which he had first washed very carefully.

The old woman, completely flabbergasted, did not take her eyes off the cossack, who took a large spoon and began to stir his soup, then to taste it.

The old woman could not help asking him, "Is it good?"

"Yes, I think it will be good in a minute, but it needs some salt. Too bad!"

"Salt? I have some salt! I can give you some."

The cossack put a little of the old woman's salt into the soup and tasted it again.

"Is it better?" asked the old woman, who never stopped watching him.

"Ah, yes, if only I could add a little handful of groats to it," sighed the cossack, still stirring his soup without lifting his nose.

"Groats? I have groats! I can give you some." And the old

woman went into her pantry to find a full sack of groats. "Here, put what you need in it," she said to him.

The cossack put in two good measures of groats, stirred again, and let his soup cook a little longer. Then he tasted it again.

"It is better yet?" asked the old woman.

"Not bad," said the cossack, "but it's a shame that you have no bacon, because with a little piece of bacon this soup would surely be much better. And if it only had an onion, it would be delicious!"

The old woman disappeared without saying a word and came back with a good big piece of bacon and an onion. The old soldier put them in his soup and continued to stir. Then he tasted it again.

"Will it be ready soon?" asked the old woman. "Is it really good now?"

"Ah, that's good soup!" exclaimed Antoniev. "All that is missing is a bit of fresh butter—then it would be a true feast!"

The old woman went out to her pantry again and came back with a piece of butter. The cossack added it to his soup, stirred it once more, and decided that it was just right and ready to be eaten.

The two of them sat down at the table on which the old woman had placed two bowls and two spoons. They started to eat the soup and found it very good indeed! Truly there was nothing missing, and the old cossack had three helpings!

"Ah, what a fine meal! I would never have believed that one could make such a good soup from an axe without a handle," exclaimed the astonished miserly woman, who had thoroughly enjoyed herself.

"Don't ever forget the recipe for axe soup!" said the clever cossack, laughing in his beard.

Kvakouchka the Frog Princess

There was once a czar who had three sons. All three were brave, handsome, and of age to take a wife.

One day the czar called them to him and said to them, "My beloved sons, before I grow old, I would like to see all three of you married. I long to look upon your wives, see you happy with them, and know my grandchildren."

His three sons—Michael, Alexis, and Igor—answered him, "It shall be as you wish, father, but whom do you desire to give us as wives?"

"I will tell you what to do," said their father. "Each one of you must take a bow with a single arrow and go out into the countryside. There you must each shoot an arrow in a different direction. Wherever your arrow falls, there your destiny awaits you."

Each of the czar's sons then took his bow and arrow and went out. Michael, the oldest, turned toward the east, drew his bow first, and shot his arrow into the air. Michael's arrow fell in the courtyard of a powerful lord, just under the window of his daughter, the beautiful Alenouchka. Alenouchka picked up the arrow and came to meet her future husband.

The second son, Alexis, turned towards the west, drew his bow, and shot his arrow into the air. His arrow fell into the garden of a rich merchant. The merchant's daughter, the lovely Sophia, who just happened to be walking there, picked it up and came to meet her future husband.

The youngest son, Igor, who was called czarevitch, turned towards the south. He drew his bow and shot his arrow into the air. Igor-czarevitch's arrow fell near a swamp and he had to walk through the mud to find it.

But Kvakouchka the frog already had the muddy arrow in her grasp. "Frog," Igor said to her, "give me back my arrow."

"No, Igor-czarevitch!" answered the frog. "You must take me as your wife!"

"What!" exclaimed Igor. "Do you think that I am going to take a frog for a wife? My father will surely let me shoot a second arrow, for I do not wish to marry you, you horrible croaker!"

But when he returned to the castle with the frog at his heels, his father said to him severely, "You must marry her, Igor-czarevitch, because fate has chosen her for you." The tone of his voice showed that there was to be no reply, and Igor had to surrender.

Soon the czar ordered three grand parties to celebrate the marriages of his sons, and all three sons, with their new wives, settled down not far from the palace.

Several days later the czar called his sons to him. "I would like to know," he said to them, "which one of you has married the woman who is most skillful at needlework. Let each one of your wives do me the honor and great pleasure to cut, sew,

and embroider for me a beautiful shirt, which you will bring me tomorrow morning."

The three sons bowed before their father. Michael, the eldest, went to see his wife, Alenouchka, who immediately set to work on a shirt. Alexis, the second son, went to see his wife, Sophia, who, without losing an instant, began to cut a shirt for the czar.

As for Igor-czarevitch, he returned home feeling very sad. He sat down near the stove and took his head in his hands. He did not dare to confide his problem to Kvakouchka the frog, whom he had taken for a wife. But Kvakouchka hopped once on the floor and asked as gently as a frog can, "Ribbit, ribbit, what is the matter, Igor-czarevitch? Won't you tell me what makes you so sad?"

"My father would like you to make him a beautiful shirt by tomorrow, Kvakouchka! And I know that you cannot do it. While I lament, my brothers' wives have already started to work."

"Why worry so, Igor-czarevitch? Rather have confidence in your wife, Kvakouchka, and get to sleep. A surprise will be waiting for you tomorrow morning!"

So Igor went off to sleep, forgetting his troubles. Then Kvakouchka threw off her frog skin and for several hours became Vassilissa the wise—so beautiful that there are not words beautiful enough to describe her. She ran out on the doorstep, clapped her hands, and called, "My nurses and nannies! Hurry! Get ready! Cut! Sew! Embroider! I need for the czar, my father-in-law, a shirt as beautiful as the ones my father wears!"

The next morning when Igor-czarevitch woke up, he saw the frog jumping on the floor and a beautiful embroidered shirt on the table.

In his joy, Igor did not forget to thank Kvakouchka. Then he took the shirt and went with it to his father, the czar. When he arrived, the czar was looking at the shirts that his other sons had brought him.

"This one," he said, unfolding the shirt that Michael had brought to him, "Is only good enough to wear in a smoky cabin! Your wife needs to take lessons on how to cut, sew, and embroider!"

"This one," he said, unfolding the shirt that Alexis had brought him, "is only good enough to hide under a fur-lined coat on a bad winter's day!"

Then Igor-czarevitch approached and unfolded before his father the most beautiful shirt he had ever seen.

"I have never worn such a beautiful shirt, not even on a festival day!" exclaimed the czar, enchanted.

As they returned home, Michael and Alexis said to each other, "We certainly were wrong to have pitied our young brother because of his bad luck! He did not marry a frog, but a magician!"

However, when their wives, Alenouchka and Sophia, learned what had happened, they felt jealousy enter their hearts.

Some time later, the czar called his sons to him once again, and said to them, "I would like to know which one of your wives can bake the best bread. Let each one of them give me the honor and great pleasure of preparing a delicious loaf of bread, which you will bring to me tomorrow morning."

The three sons bowed before their father. Michael went to see his wife, Alenouchka, who found her best recipe and immediately began to mix the flour, water, and leavening together. Alexis went to see his wife, Sophia, who also soon set to work, kneading the dough in her kneading trough.

As for Igor-czarevitch, he went home very sadly. He sat down near the stove and took his head in his hands. He did not dare to confide his grief to Kvakouchka the frog, whom he had been forced to take as a wife. But Kvakouchka hopped twice on the floor and asked as nicely as a frog can, "Ribbit, ribbit, what is the matter with you, Igor-czarevitch? Will you not tell me what makes you so sad?"

"My father would like you to make a beautiful loaf of bread

for tomorrow, Kvakouchka, and I know you cannot do it. My brothers' wives are already busy kneading the dough!"

"Why worry, Igor-czarevitch? Rather have confidence in your wife, Kvakouchka, and go to sleep. Tomorrow a surprise will await you!"

So Igor forgot his troubles and went to bed. Then Kvakouchka threw off her frog skin again and became for a while Vassilissa the wise—beautiful beyond description, even in a fairy tale.

Quickly she ran out on the doorstep of her house, clapped her hands, and called, "My nannies and nurses! Hurry! Get ready! Weigh! Knead! Bake! I need for the czar, my father-in-law, a bread as white, as tender, as crusty as the ones I used to eat in my father's palace!"

The next morning when Igor woke up, he saw the frog on the floor and a magnificent golden bread, perfectly baked and glazed, on the table.

In his joy, he did not forget to thank Kvakouchka. Then he took the bread and carried it still warm to his father, the czar. The czar was already receiving from his other sons the breads that their wives had baked.

"This bread," he said to his oldest son, "is not sufficiently raised. It is only good enough to dip into cabbage soup!" And he sent it back to the kitchen.

"This bread," he said to his second son, "is burned without being baked. It is only good enough to feed to the chickens!" And he sent it out to the hen house!

Then Igor-czarevitch approached and put before his father exactly the bread the czar wanted—white, tender, crusty, baked exactly right, and beautifully glazed!

"I have never tasted, not even for the feast of Easter, bread so beautiful to look at and so good to eat!" exclaimed the czar, delighted.

Some time later, the czar had his three sons come to him once more and he invited them to a party which he was giving at the palace the next day. He asked them to extend his invitation to their wives also.

While the beautiful Alenouchka was busy thinking of the brocade and silk dress that she would wear the next evening, and while the beautiful Sophia was also beginning to get ready for the party, Igor-czarevitch returned home very sadly. He sat down near the stove and took his head in his hands. He did not dare to confide his despair to Kvakouchka the frog, whom he had been forced to take for a wife.

"Ribbit, ribbit," she said as she hopped three times on the floor, "what is the matter dear Igor-czarevitch? Can you not tell your wife, who has already helped you out of two embarrassing situations?"

"My father would like us to attend the grand party he is giving in his palace tomorrow evening. But how will I dare show you to all the guests alongside of beautiful Alenouchka and lovely Sophia?"

"Why be troubled, Igor-czarevitch? Have confidence in your wife, Kvakouchka, one more time. Go to the party yourself. And wait for me. When you hear a tremendous clap of thunder, do not be afraid, and reassure our sisters-in-law. Tell them simply, 'Don't be alarmed, it is my frog-wife who is arriving!' "

The next day Igor-czarevitch dressed in his most beautiful clothes and went alone to the party.

As soon as they saw him, the beautiful Alenouchka and the lovely Sophia, who were angry at having been judged poorer housekeepers than Kvakouchka the frog, rushed forward to show themselves to Igor-czarevitch in all their beautiful attire, adorned, painted, and perfumed. Then they started to laugh and make fun of Igor's wife.

"Why didn't your wife come, Igor-czarevitch? Why didn't you bring her in your well-folded handkerchief? Such a perfect wife! We would have been delighted to see her! One would think that you are afraid of losing her and of seeing her return forever to her swamp!"

A handsome cloth, embroidered all over with golden threads, covered the party table. And on the table seven settings of gilded silver had been placed—one for the czar and one for each of his sons and daughters-in law. But just as everyone—except Kvakouchka the frog—sat down at the beautiful table, a terribly loud clap of thunder shook the entire palace.

Everyone jumped at the sudden noise and Alenouchka and Sophia, trembling with fear, began to flee. But Igor-czarevitch said to them calmly, "Don't be afraid, dear sisters-in-law. It is only my little frog-wife who is arriving for the party!"

And at that very moment a carriage drawn by six white horses stopped at the gates of the palace. But no ugly frog jumped out. Instead Vassilissa the wise appeared in all her

beauty. Her dress of emerald green was decorated with silver
water lilies and a crescent moon shone in her golden hair.

Igor-czarevitch took her hand and showed her to the place
that was reserved for her, and the festivities began. The beautiful Alenouchka and the lovely Sophia could not take their
eyes off their magnificent sister-in-law. Igor-czarevitch
beamed with joy, and his father and brothers were astounded.

Creamed breasts of swan were served, accompanied by
delicious wines. Vassilissa ate her breast of swan, and then
she thrust several small swan bones into the folds of her left
sleeve. When she had sipped as much wine as she cared for,
she threw the rest into the folds of her right sleeve.

Alenouchka and Sophia watched their sister-in-law with
astonishment. Of course they decided to do just as Vassilissa
the wise had done, thinking it would bring them good luck.

After the meal, at the first chords of the balalaikas, Vassilissa stood up, astounding the guests by her striking beauty.
Taking Igor-czarevitch by the hand, she pulled him into a

wonderfully gay and lively dance. Then with a wide sweep of her right hand, she shook her sleeve and made a blue lake appear on the grounds of the palace, And with a wide sweep of her left hand, she shook her sleeve and put three white swans into the lake!

Naturally the wives of the older sons wanted to do the same. But with their right hands they sent forth only wine, which splashed the guests; and with their left hands they scattered only swan bones, which did not at all please the czar!

However, the celebration continued joyously and lasted long into the night. And while the czar danced with Vassilissa, Igor-czarevitch went quietly home. As he expected, he found the frog skin abandoned in a corner. Without hesitation, he threw it into the fire and joyfully watched it consumed by the flames.

At that moment, Vassilissa the wise came home in her carriage drawn by its six white horses. She immediately started to look all about for her frog skin and was terribly upset when she could not find it.

"Alas, Igor-czarevitch! Alas! What have you done? If you had waited just three more days, I would have been yours forever. Now I must leave you, and you are going to have to look for me throughout thirty countries and across forty kingdoms! You will wear out nine pairs of boots with iron soles before you have me in your arms again if you succeed at last — and if I am still waiting for you!"

And Vassilissa, in tears, changed herself into a gray seagull and flew out the window, while her carriage and its six white horses disappeared!

Igor-czarevitch wept for a long time, a very long time. Then he left his house and went to look for his wife, Vassilissa the wise.

Did he travel far, very far? Did he walk for a long time, a very long time? No one really knows. But by the time he met a little old man on the road, Igor's boots were already very worn, his tunic torn, and his hat softened by the rain.

"Good-day, Igor-czarevitch!" the little old man, bent with age, called out to him. "Whom are you looking for and where are you going? Perhaps I can help you; at my age I know so many things!"

"Ah, little old man," answered Igor-czarevitch, "I have lost Vassilissa the wise through my own fault and I cannot find her!"

"Indeed, Igor-czarevitch, you have been neither wise nor patient," the little old man said to him severely. "Why did you burn the skin of Kvakouchka the frog? It was not you who was wearing it. You had no right to get rid of it. But let me tell you what I know, and listen to me well, for there is perhaps still time for you to find your wife, Vassilissa the wise. First I must tell you that she is the daughter of the Eternal Magician. She was so beautiful a young girl that her father was jealous of her. He changed her into a frog for three years. By burning her frog skin you have prolonged the evil spell. And now it will not be easy for you to find Vassilissa, for her father will change her appearance constantly to punish you. Here, take this ball of twine, throw it in front of you and wherever it rolls, follow it boldly. Good-luck, Igor-czarevitch!"

Igor thanked the old man and started off on his journey. He must surely have walked an extraordinarily long way for he had to change his boots several times.

One evening he was astonished to find in front of his ball of twine, a curious little cabin perched on top of chicken legs! The cabin kept turning round and round on its strange legs. Igor-czarevitch cried out, "Cabin, little cabin, stop turning like that! Stay in one place for me. Turn your back to the forest and show me your face!"

Immediately the little cabin turned its door towards Igor and ceased turning.

Igor-czarevitch pushed the door open and went in. On a stove built of nine bricks was seated Baba-Yaga, the sorceress! Igor had never seen her before, but he recognized her immediately. Her teeth, enormous and pointed, like the teeth of a saw, hung down to the floor and her hooked nose darkened the entire cabin!

"Tsk! Tsk!" she said through her jaws. "What on earth do I see before me? A Russian in the flesh and bone! Why have you come here to me? Who sent you?"

"I am looking for Vassilissa the wise, who is my wife," answered Igor innocently. "My ball of twine led me to your cabin, Baba-Yaga."

"What a pity for you, Igor-czarevitch! And why did you take so long to come? Vassilissa the wise is still under the power of the Eternal Magician, and they say that she has completely forgotten you! She is now at the home of my oldest sister. Go there quickly; your ball of twine will lead you. But remember well what I say to you — the power of the Eternal Magician is such that as soon as you enter the cabin, Vassilissa will change into a spindle and my sister will spin threads of gold with this spindle. Grab the spindle from her hands immediately! Break it in two and throw one piece in front of you and the other behind you. I cannot tell you any more."

Igor-czarevitch thanked Baba-Yaga and started on his journey at daybreak. How long did he walk and how far did he go? No one knows, not even the sorceress Baba-Yaga, but he wore out three more pairs of boots with iron soles! Then one evening he saw another little cabin perched on top of chicken legs. This cabin also kept turning round and round on its curious legs.

Igor cried out, "Cabin, little cabin, stop turning! Stay in your place as you should. Turn your back to the forest and show me your face!"

Immediately the little cabin stopped turning and showed its door.

Igor-czarevitch pushed the door open and went in. On a stove built of nine bricks was seated an old sorceress as horri-

ble to look at as Baba-Yaga. She was busy spinning threads of gold with her spindle. As soon as she saw Igor enter, she started to whistle through her large teeth.

"Tsk! Tsk! Why did you come to my cabin, Igor-czarevitch?" And as she spoke, she got up, immediately put her spindle into a drawer, and started to lock it. Igor, remembering the words of Baba-Yaga, quickly pulled open the drawer, seized the spindle, and with one swift blow, broke it in two. He threw one piece in front of him and the other behind him.

At once Vassilissa the wise appeared before him exactly as he had seen her at the palace of the czar, resplendent in her emerald green dress decorated with silver water lilies, and wearing a crescent moon in her golden hair!

"Ah, Igor-czarevitch! How long it has taken you to come!" she said, throwing herself into his arms. "Thanks to your courage, my father, the Eternal Magician, has finally freed me from his evil spell and I have forgiven you for having burned my frog skin. Never again will I be Kvakouchka the frog for you or for anyone!"

Then the sorceress and the cabin on its chicken legs vanished and Vassilissa's carriage appeared, drawn by its six white horses.

Igor-czarevitch, all his fatigue forgotten, got into the carriage with his beautiful wife. Three days later they arrived in their own country. The czar was delighted to see his son and daughter-in-law again, and in their honor he ordered a sumptuous banquet. Igor was happy to see his two older brothers with the beautiful Alenouchka and the lovely Sophia once more.

All sorrow and jealousy were now forgotten, and Vassilissa the very wise and Igor-czarevitch lived together happily for a very long time.

A Strange Judgement

On each side of the Smorodina River lived two neighbors who barely managed to get along. To the south was the cabin and land of Gavrilo; in the north was the cabin and the land of Danilo.

One year the harvest was bad for Gavrilo. With winter coming on, he had to sell his horse to buy food, and as the winter was very cold, he burned his firewood quickly and soon had none left.

So he went into the forest to cut wood to warm his cabin, but he wondered how he was going to get it back home now that he no longer had a horse.

"Bah!" he said to himself, "Danilo will surely lend me his!" And leaving his pile of wood, he went to knock at Danilo's door. But Danilo, who had a good harvest and had saved up quite a few rubles, did not really want to help his neighbor, who he knew was in trouble.

"Take my horse for today," he said to him, "but return it to me tomorrow in good condition! And after tomorrow be on your way!"

Gavrilo returned home with Danilo's horse and wanted to harness it to his sleigh. But then he remembered that he no longer had a collar or a harness! He had sold everything with his horse for several rubles more.

"What bad luck!" he exclaimed, "and I cannot return to my neighbor to ask him to lend me his. I am going to attach my sleigh securely to the tail of Danilo's horse. In this way the horse will be able to pull enough wood to warm my cabin."

And that is what he did. But just before arriving home, the sled hit a stump. Gavrilo, tired and in a hurry to get home, did not pay any attention. Instead he whipped the horse to make him move faster. Whereupon the horse bounded off at a gallop leaving his tail still attached to Gavrilo's sled!

Feeling himself free, the horse galloped back home to the other side of the Smorodina River. When his master saw that his horse no longer had a tail, he became terribly angry.

"Danilo will pay for this!" he screamed. "I'm going to bring him to justice." And he went to court to make a complaint against his neighbor.

Thus it was that Gavrilo and Danilo were called before Judge Ladislas.

As he walked toward the village, poor Gavrilo said to himself, "I have never been in court in my life, for I know too well the proverb that says, 'If you are weak among the strong, do not fight! If you are poor among the rich, do not argue!' Alas, poor Gavrilo," he mourned, "they will condemn you!"

Meanwhile, the rich Danilo galloped towards the city on his horse without a tail.

All the time he was sadly lamenting to himself, Gavrilo did not notice that he was crossing a frozen stream on a wooden

bridge which did not have a hand rail. He walked too near the edge, took a false step, and fell. At that very moment a sleigh loaded with an enormous barrel of vodka was passing under the bridge!

Poor Gavrilo fell directly onto the barrel and smashed it completely. Luckily, though, he did not hurt himself at all.

"I will take you to court for making me lose all my vodka!" yelled the furious merchant.

Poor Gavrilo, who was on his way to court anyhow, continued along in the company of the merchant.

"Alas, Gavrilo!" he said to himself. "It is possible that you will be condemned twice, poor as you are!" And he felt completely helpless and hopeless.

Just then his eye fell on a big, highly polished stone lying at the edge of the road. He let the merchant go on ahead of him and bent down to pick up the stone, which he hid under his tunic.

"This way," he said to himself, "the judge will see my big stomach. He will think I must be very rich to eat so well that I have such a great big stomach. And if he wishes to condemn me in spite of that, I will be able to hit him with the stone and kill him."

They all arrived at court—the merchant, who had lost all his vodka; the rich neighbor, whose horse had lost its tail; and poor Gavrilo, who had nothing to lose.

Judge Ladislas started to question the rich man, the poor man, and the merchant before making the judgement. It was the moment for Gavrilo to act, otherwise he had no chance of winning. So he showed the judge that he had something important hidden under his tunic, and he murmured, "Judge Ladislas, before judging me, take a look at what I have here!"

Gavrilo did this three times. Each time the judge delayed his decision and started to think, "What is that man trying to show me? Gold? Why not?" He looked once again. "Perhaps it is only some silver? At any rate there is a lot of it! Let's judge him accordingly then!"

He took his time and judged the two affairs accordingly.

"Gavrilo, the accused, is to take this horse and keep it until its tail has grown back." he decided. "And the merchant is to bring another barrel of vodka and let himself fall off the bridge at that same place so we may know if he told the truth."

And that was the judge's decision!

Then the rich neighbor, Danilo, declared, "If that's the way things are going to be, give me back my horse the way he is, Gavrilo! Since I will never attach my sled to his tail, it won't bother me!"

"No, neighbor," answered Gavrilo, "we must do as the judge has ordered. I will keep your horse. I will keep him for as long as it takes for his tail to grow back!"

Then Danilo began to beg, "I will give you thirty rubles if you give my horse back to me!"

"At that price it is out of the question!" Gavrilo dared to say.

"Sixty rubles then. But give him back to me!" pleaded Danilo.

"All right, sixty!" accepted Gavrilo.

So the rich man paid sixty rubles and took his horse away with him. Then the merchant said to Gavrilo, "Listen, I forgive you, for I certainly do not want to risk breaking my bones and losing a second barrel of vodka!"

"But what are you saying, merchant? What the judge ordered, you must do! Go get your vodka and jump off the bridge. I will be there to watch you."

"I would rather give you one hundred rubles right now!"

"As you wish," answered Gavrilo, and he put the one hundred rubles in his pocket on top of the sixty.

At this moment, Gavrilo thought that he had done very well, and was getting ready to leave, when the judge called for him. He had not forgotten that Gavrilo was hiding something under his tunic.

"Give me what you showed me!" he ordered.

"If you wish, Judge Ladislas, and only if you are not afraid of being disappointed!" And from his tunic Gavrilo took the stone and placed it in front of the judge, happy to be rid of it because it was so heavy.

"It was this stone that I showed you," he said to the judge, "and if you had found me guilty, I was ready to kill you with it!"

The judge dismissed him and said to himself, "I judged this man well! For if I had found him guilty, I would not be alive now!"

As for Gavrilo, he left the stone with the judge and happily went off to buy himself a horse, a harness, and even a barrel of vodka!

The Legend of the Salty Sea

Once there were two brothers, Vlasios and Leonid. Life had brought neither luck nor fortune to Vlasios, who was very poor. As for Leonid, he ignored all those who were not as rich as he, and he never wanted to see Vlasios for fear that his poor brother might beg him for something.

One year, as the Easter festival approached, there was truly nothing left to eat at Vlasios' house. Natacha, his wife, said to him sadly, "What will we do for Easter, Vlasios? We have neither meat in the salting tub, nor poultry in the hen house. The merchant will no longer give us credit. Your brother Leonid killed his ox yesterday, surely he would not refuse to give you a piece of the meat."

Poor Vlasios wanted to please his wife, and he went to knock at the door of his brother, the rich Leonid.

"Happy Easter, my brother!" he said to him. "It is my wife, Natacha, who sends me. All we have left to eat for the Easter holiday is a little black bread. We know that you have killed your ox and I have come to ask you for a piece of the meat."

But Leonid's heart was hard, even on festival days. He asked his servant to bring him one of the hooves of the ox that he had just killed. He gave it to Vlasios saying spitefully, "Here! Here is something for Natacha and you! And go to the devil with it!"

Poor Vlasios did not have the courage to return home with an ox's hoof with which one could do nothing. Instead he went towards the forest and as he walked, he said to himself, "Since my brother said 'go to the devil with it,' I will take this ox's hoof to Satan!"

So he went into the forest and walked and walked for a very long time. Finally he met three woodcutters who asked, "Vlasios, where are you going all alone in the forest, instead of preparing for the holiday?"

"I am going to Satan's house. I am bringing him this ox's hoof," answered Vlasios. "You know the forest well; do you know where I will find the devil's house?"

"Sure we know!" answered the three woodcutters all together. "Walk straight ahead, keep going without stopping, without turning or returning, and you will arrive at Satan's house this evening! But listen to us carefully — in exchange for this hoof, Satan is going to offer you silver."

"Silver!" exclaimed Vlasios, who no longer had even one ruble.

"Yes, silver! But be careful, Vlasios! You must not accept Satan's silver, and if he then offers you gold, you must not take that either."

"But what will I ask him for in exchange?" asked Vlasios, very disappointed.

"You will simply ask him to give you his hand mill."

"His hand mill!" repeated Vlasios. "But I don't need a hand mill; I have nothing to grind."

Just listen to our advice, Vlasios! You will not be sorry," answered the woodcutters, who then went back to their work.

So poor Vlasios walked straight ahead until evening, and finally he saw a little black cabin. It had to be the devil's home. He pushed open the door and went in. Inside sat Satan, who seemed to be waiting for him.

"What have you brought to me, Vlasios?" asked Satan at once. "Woe unto you if your gift does not please me!"

"The hoof of an ox!" declared Vlasios, who was in a very tight spot.

"Show it to me," demanded Satan, "for I am very often promised and very seldom satisfied."

"Here it is," said Vlasios.

Satan took the ox hoof and bit into it heartily, and in three mouthfuls swallowed it!

"Ugh!" he grimaced. "Its been three hundred years since I've last eaten that! By Hades it isn't too bad! What would you say, Vlasios, to these two fistfuls of silver as payment?"

And the poor man answered, "No, Satan, I do not need any silver."

Then Satan took a bag of gold pieces and said to Vlasios, "I will give you two fistfuls of gold if you want them."

"No, Satan, I do not need any gold either."

"But what *do* you need then? I have eaten the ox hoof which you brought to me. I really must pay you, peasant!"

"I want your hand mill," answered Vlasios who could not take his eyes off the bags filled with gold and silver.

"My hand mill!" cried the devil, "but what for?"

"I don't know, Satan, but you are going to tell me!"

"Very well," said Satan. "Listen to me carefully. The mill which I am going to give you is not an ordinary mill. It can do anything that you command it to. All you need to do is say, 'Grind mill, grind!' and it will grind anything you want. When you have enough, simply say to it, 'Mill of Satan! Stop grinding this instant!' and your mill will stop. Now take it and be gone!" exclaimed Satan.

Vlasios thanked Satan and started home with his mill under his arm. The road to his cabin was long and the mill was heavy. Poor Vlasios would have to spend the entire night trudging through the forest.

Soon the rain started to fall, the wind started to blow, and the branches of the trees slapped him in the face. Vlasios walked as quickly as he could. It seemed to him that Satan was following him to take back his mill. Finally, at daybreak he arrived at his cabin where Natacha, who had worried about him all day and all night, was waiting for him.

"Where were you?" she asked him. "Could your brother Leonid have entertained you all this time, and could you have forgotten me?"

But Vlasios answered her, "I went to see Satan and here is the present I have for you!" he put the hand mill on the table and pronounced the magic words, "Grind, mill, grind all that we need for the Easter holiday!"

And before the eyes of the dazed couple, the mill started to turn all by itself on the table, grinding out everything they needed—flour, sugar, groats, meat, fish! Never had Natacha seen so much food! When she had filled all the bags, all the pots, and all the bowls she possessed, Vlasios cried out, "Mill of Satan! Stop grinding this instant!" and the mill stopped immediately.

Then Natacha kneaded her dough, warmed up her stove for the cakes, put the fish in a cauldron and the meats in a stew pan. The Easter festival was celebrated as joyously by the poor couple as it was by all their richer neighbors.

And from that moment on, there was never again anything lacking in the home of Vlasios and Natacha.

One day Vlasios ordered his mill to grind several measures of oats and he brought them to his horse which was in front of the house. At that moment Leonid, the rich brother, was passing by with his horses and servants. When his horses saw the freshly ground oats, the servants could not keep them from coming up and eating some.

When Leonid saw that, he exclaimed, "Hey there, grooms, don't let my horses do that! They might eat some filth and get sick!"

The grooms brought back the horses and said to their master, "No, master, your brother's horses eat excellent oats. And everyone except you knows that your brother has become rich. He has everything he wants—and lots of it!"

Leonid's curiosity was aroused. He immediately decided to visit his brother.

"How have you suddenly become so rich? Who gives you all this? Where do you get it all?" Leonid asked his brother.

Poor Vlasios was so happy now that he did not think for a moment to hide his joy from his brother. He simply said to him, "Well, a little before the Easter holidays you gave me an ox hoof and told me to bring it to the devil. That is just what I did! I found out where Satan lived, and I gave him the hoof. I would accept neither the gold nor the silver that he offered me, but asked him instead for his mill. It is the mill which gives me absolutely anything I want."

"Show it to me!" exclaimed the brother, who was greedy and envious.

"If you wish," answered the good Vlasios, who went to fetch the mill. He then asked it to give him all sorts of delicious things for his brother. The mill started to turn immediately, and the table became filled with roast beef, legs of lamb, wines, and vodka!

The rich Leonid opened his eyes wide with astonishment and envy. He cried out, "Sell me that mill!"

"No, it is not for sale. I need it for myself," Vlasios replied firmly.

But the rich Leonid kept on insisting, finally offering all his wealth to his brother for possession of the mill.

"I will not sell it!" Vlasios, who did not change his mind, always answered.

Then Leonid, seeing that he was not getting anywhere, tried something else. "How ungrateful you are, my brother! Tell me, have you forgotten who gave you that ox hoof?"

"It was you."

"There, you see! You owe me your gratitude for that. Since you do not want to sell me your mill, you cannot refuse to lend it to me for a while."

Then Vlasios, after thinking it over for a minute, agreed, and the rich Leonid was very happy. He immediately took the mill and returned home. Now Leonid knew how to tell the mill to grind—but he had forgotten to ask how to stop it!

The next day he went off to sea in his boat taking the mill with him.

"At this time," he said to himself, "people are salting fish. Salt is very expensive. I am going to sell salt! Lots of salt!"

He commanded the mill just as he should, "Grind, my mill, grind! Give me lots of salt!"

And the mill started to turn and produced quantities of very pure, very white salt, the kind that sells the best. Seeing this, Leonid, mad with joy, already calculated the profits he was going to make and he continued to cry out, "Grind, mill! Grind without stopping!"

The pile of salt got bigger and bigger. It was past time to tell the mill to stop, but the rich Leonid had lost his head and he continued to order the mill to grind more and more!

Under the weight of the salt, the boat sunk deeper into the water, almost up to the prow. The water was rapidly filling the boat and it was about to sink.

Finally Leonid came to his senses and started to shout, "Stop grinding! Stop immediately!" But these were the wrong words and the mill continued to grind beautiful white salt without stopping!

"Stop!" the wicked Leonid cried again. But the mill did not stop grinding and would never stop.

The boat and the greedy Leonid sank to the bottom of the sea. The rich man perished and the sea swallowed him up.

From that time on, the mill has never stopped turning. It still continues to grind good salt. That is why sea water is always salty.

Igor the Poor Man and Boris the Rich Man

Once long ago there lived on the great steppe of Russia, Igor the poor man. He possessed nothing except his horse and his tent. But he was joyous, intelligent, clever, and inventive.

On the other side of the same steppe lived Boris the rich man. He possessed much wealth, many magnificent tents, numerous horses, flocks of sheep, and all that could make a man happy! But Boris was never happy because he was miserly, so miserly that he always lived in anguish.

It was said of him that he even refused to give a piece of bread or a glass of water to those who came to visit him. It was also said that his wife, Vanessa, was as miserly as he, and that his daughter, Alène, was breathtakingly beautiful.

One day, Igor the poor man wanted to know if everything

they said about this Boris was true, and he decided to visit him. So he folded his tent, put it up on his horse's back, and started off.

"Are you going off to seek your fortune, Igor the poor man?" asked everyone he met.

"I am going to get myself invited to Boris the rich man's tent" cried Igor into the wind of the steppe as he galloped along, "for I no longer have anything to eat at home, and nothing more to do here!"

"Well, then, hearty appetite!" answered his friends. "But don't count too heavily on Boris the rich man to entertain you with fat lambs and delicious wines!"

"Sure, sure, we shall see!" exclaimed Igor.

He traveled a long time across the steppe, looking for the tent of Boris the rich man, and each time he asked his way, he was told, "Go further, much further! Do not look for the home of Boris the miser here! He wanted to live where no one would come to bother him!"

So Igor continued his journey until finally he noticed at the other end of the steppe, an isolated tent surrounded on all sides by reeds.

"Ah hah!" he thought immediately. "It is not by chance that this Boris has settled in the middle of the reeds! He did that so he can know in advance if any visitor is approaching his tent. At night the noise of the reeds must wake him up. And during the day, if he sees the stems move, he knows that someone is approaching and he has time to hide all his food as quickly as possible. That way he is not obliged to offer any to his visitor!"

Then Igor, clever and sly as he was, began to seek a way to pass through the reeds without a sound in order to surprise Boris the rich man.

"Impossible to cross without making a sound!" he concluded. But he had already thought of a trick. He got down from his horse and began to pick up stones — lots of stones!

Still undiscovered, he waited for night to fall. Then he threw a stone and the reeds began to rustle. Immediately

Boris bounded out of his tent, looked all around, saw nothing, and went back inside.

Igor threw a second stone. Again the reeds started to rustle. Again Boris went out to look around.

"Who goes there?" he cried. No one answered, and he went back into his tent.

But Igor threw a third stone. Again the reeds began to rustle and Boris went out again—no one!

"It's the wind that shakes the reeds!" Boris said, to reassure himself. And when Igor threw a fourth stone, Boris no longer bothered to leave his tent.

That was exactly what Igor was waiting for. He took his horse by the bridle and broke a path through the reeds right up to the door of the miser's tent. Once he arrived there, he raised the tent flap and looked inside. How crowded everything was under the tent! There were rugs and cushions and

boxes piled one on top of the other. Igor could hardly believe his eyes!

Standing in front of the fire, Boris was busy stirring something that was cooking in a large cauldron. By the aroma, Igor recognized lamb stew. He saw Boris taste it, then put the cover back on the cauldron to let it cook some more. Then Boris started to prepare a sausage.

In the back of the tent, Boris's wife kneaded dough while her daughter plucked a goose. A servant approached the fire to singe the head of the lamb.

Igor had seen enough. He could not wait any longer. Suddenly he entered the tent saying, "Greetings to you, people of the steppe!"

Whereupon Boris sat on the sausage he was preparing, his wife sat on the dough she was kneading, his daughter hid the goose she was plucking under the pillow, and the servant hid the lamb's head he was singeing behind his back!

Finally Boris greeted Igor and spoke to him, "What news of the steppe do you bring to us, stranger?"

"Oh, many interesting things and many astonishing things. I could not tell you everything!"

"If you cannot tell us everything, at least begin by telling us something!"

"Very well," said Igor. "While I was approaching your tent I saw a snake crawling."

"Was it big?" asked Boris.

"Big enough, but not as big as the sausage on which you are sitting this minute, Boris the rich man."

Boris did not say anything, but his brow darkened.

"You can believe me," continued Igor, "the head of this snake was big and black, but much smaller than the head of the lamb which your servant was singeing when I entered and which is now behind his back!"

Boris the miser raised his eyebrows, but said nothing, and Igor continued his story.

"Well, this snake crawled along, and while it crawled it whistled a little like the vapor of the cauldron in which you are cooking your lamb stew this evening! Of course, I jumped off my horse, and I crushed the head of the serpent with a single blow of a stone. But do you know what his crushed head looked like, Boris?"

"No!" said Boris.

"Like the dough on which your wife is seated! These are some of the astonishing things that I have seen on the steppe," concluded Igor. "If I am lying, then I am waiting to be plucked exactly as your beautiful daughter was plucking that goose a little while ago!"

Boris was angry. That was very plain. However, he did not chase Igor from his tent, but neither did he propose to share his meal with him. He simply invited him to spend the night, and they sat talking very late into the evening.

The cauldron continued to cook, spreading a delicious aroma of lamb cooked to perfection. Igor, who was famished, could not keep his eyes off it and his mouth was watering! But the miser who seemed to have noticed nothing, suddenly said, "Bubble, my cauldron, bubble! You can continue to cook for six months!"

"Very well," Igor said to himself, "since that's the way things are, why stay awake so late!"

And he immediately took off his boots, stretched, yawned very loudly, and exclaimed, "And you, my boots, you can rest here for two years! It's very nice here!"

With this, he stretched out to go to sleep.

When Boris the miser realized that his unexpected guest had no intention of leaving, he signaled to his family to go to bed without supper, because for nothing in the world would he wish to share his good meal with this Igor—nor anyone else either!

"When this intruder is asleep," he thought, "I will awaken my family and we will eat the lamb stew."

As for Igor, clever and famished as he was, he promised himself that he would eat to his heart's content as soon as Boris fell asleep! How strange, he thought, to sleep without eating, especially when the lamb in its cauldron was already cooked to perfection. Boris must truly be miserly to prefer to go to bed with an empty stomach, rather than share his lamb stew with a hungry traveler. Igor himself was so hungry, he could not possibly have fallen asleep!

Soon he heard Boris's deep and regular snoring. Now he would be able to get up and eat at last!

Without a sound, he raised the cover on the cauldron and began eating the lamb. He finished almost all of it, so great was his hunger! And then he threw into the cauldron the sleeping miser's boots to take the place of the meat he had just eaten. He carefully put the cover back on the cauldron, stretched out, and waited, making believe that he was sleeping.

After a while, Boris woke up. He looked carefully at Igor, bent his ear towards him, and decided that he was surely sleeping. Being very careful, he went to wake his wife and daughter who were sleeping in another part of the tent.

"Quickly! Wake up! Don't make any noise! The three of us are going to eat this lamb while Igor is asleep!"

Boris raised the cover of the cauldron and put it down without making a sound. He took his boots out, not recognizing them, cut them in pieces, served his wife and daughter — and did not forget himself! All three began to eat, and chewed and chewed and chewed, without being able to swallow a thing.

"What is this? What's going on here? Why has this good meat become so tough? It's surely the fault of that intruder, Igor! Did I invite him here? It's his fault that this lamb has gotten so tough because it was kept cooking and recooking," said Boris. "But that doesn't matter; when Igor leaves we will find a way to eat this lamb. We must not waste any of it. Let's pick up the pieces and put them back in the cauldron."

Then Vanessa, Boris's wife, quickly prepared some cakes with the dough she had kneaded the night before, and put them on the fire to cook. As soon as they were done, without even leaving them time to cool, Boris stuffed them into his shirt and went off to watch over his flocks because it was already daybreak.

But Igor, who was not sleeping at all, had seen everything, and the odor of the cakes had hardly displeased him. When he saw the miser leave, he bounded out of the tent and joined him at a run.

"Boris, wait for me! I want to say goodbye to you for I am leaving this morning."

And he started to embrace Boris like an old friend. He squeezed him so hard that the hidden cakes began to burn Boris's chest horribly!

At first the miser did not say anything; he endured the pain for he did not want to show Igor his good cakes. But suddenly he could no longer stand the burning and he started to cry out. "I'm burning, I'm burning! Oh my cakes! Cool off or I will throw you away!" And he tore open his shirt to get rid of the cakes.

"May the dogs burn themselves on you!" he shouted angrily. But his stomach was still empty.

"Why do you give those hot cakes to your dogs?" asked Igor. "Now that they are cooler, I could surely eat them!"

Igor seized the cakes, and ate them right under the nose of the dazed Boris. "These cakes that your wife made are very good! I don't understand why you threw them to the dogs. Believe me, I have not eaten any as good for a long time!"

The miser, who still hadn't eaten anything, said nothing. He went off into the steppe to watch over his flocks. In the evening, when he came back into his tent, whom did he see sitting on his cushions? Igor the poor man who was still there!

"But you said goodbye to me this morning! You must leave!" exclaimed Boris the miser as soon as he saw Igor.

"It is true, I wanted to leave, but I am so comfortable here with you that I have changed my mind," Igor, the unwelcome guest, answered calmly.

The next morning before leaving for the steppe, and while his guest was still in bed, Boris said very softly to his wife, "Prepare a gourd full of mead for me, but be careful that Igor doesn't notice it."

Vanessa filled the gourd and gave it to him and Boris immediately hid it under his caftan.

"This time he did not see me! All is well!" he congratulated himself as he left his tent and went towards his flocks.

But he was mistaken! At that very moment Igor left the tent and started running to catch up with him. He pressed Boris in his arms even harder than the day before. He pressed him and pressed him so hard that the gourd finally burst and the mead started to flow over his caftan!

Boris flew into a fit of anger, and to get rid of Igor he threw him his gourd saying, "Here, drink! Drink! And may I see you no more!"

"Good," said Igor, "since you tell me to drink, I drink. I'm not going to insult you by refusing such a good drink. Your wife, Vanessa, certainly knows how to make mead!" And he drank what was left in the gourd to the last drop.

Just like the day before, Boris the rich man had been obliged to give Igor the poor man everything he was trying to hide. Full of anger, he went into the steppe to watch his flocks. Meanwhile Igor, the clever one, returned to the tent to chat with Vanessa, Boris's wife, and his beautiful daughter, Alène.

Igor stayed on at the miser's, always finding a way to feed himself at Boris's expense. But from evening to morning, from morning to evening, Boris kept searching for a way to get rid of his guest and at the same time get his revenge.

Finally an idea came to him. Igor possessed only his horse, and Boris decided to kill this horse, which was easily recognizable because of the white spot it had on its forehead.

But seeing Boris staring at his horse, Igor guessed his intentions. That evening before going to bed, he took some soot and smeared it over the white spot on his horse's forehead. He then took some chalk and traced a similar white spot on the forehead of Boris's best horse. When he had finished he went to bed and fell asleep.

Then Boris, in his turn, went out of the tent without awakening anyone, killed the horse marked with a white spot, and went back to bed.

In the morning he started to shout, "Igor! Something terrible has happened to your horse! I found him dead!"

But of course, Igor was not the least upset, and from the tent he called out, "Don't worry about my horse, Boris! He is just fine!"

And it was only when he went to saddle his swiftest horse and found it dead, that Boris understood that he had killed it himself. He almost died of rage.

From that moment on, Igor wanted to return to the other side of the great steppe and once again set up his tent there. But he decided that he would not leave alone. He would take with him the most beautiful young girl on the steppes of Russia, Alène, the daughter of Boris and Vanessa, whom he had loved since the first day he saw her. He knew that Alène loved him also for she did not take her eyes off him.

"I am going to take her for my wife," he said to himself, "before she becomes miserly and wicked like her father."

One morning, at the moment when Boris was getting ready to leave the tent as he usually did, Igor said to him, "Well, Boris, it is now time for me to return to the country I love on the other side of the great steppe. This evening when you return, there will be more room in your tent!"

Boris was so happy to hear that Igor was finally leaving that he could find no words to speak.

"But my boots are all worn out," added Igor. "You must give me your Alène!" Igor knew that the word *alène* also meant an awl with which to sew the leather of boots, and he guessed that

Boris would understand it as such, too. But in Igor's heart, Alène was the name of the girl whom he loved and whom he was going to take away from her miserly father, thanks to this play on words.

"Very well! Very well!" Boris answered him, delighted to be rid of him. "Take my *alène* and keep it."

This promise made, Boris went out into the steppe and Igor went back to the tent to ask Vanessa to give him her daughter, Alène.

"But you have lost your mind!" cried Vanessa. "Do you believe that we are going to give you our daughter simply because you ask for her?"

"Your husband has already given her to me! If you do not believe me, go ask him."

Then Vanessa ran out and called to her husband, "Is it true that you promised to give Igor our Alène?"

"It's true! It's true! Give it to him and let him be gone with it as quickly as possible!"

And delighted with the idea of Igor's departure, Boris whipped his horse and raced off.

His wife did not dare disobey him. She therefore let Igor take Alène, whom he loved tenderly, away with him.

And so the two young people mounted the horse with the white spot and set off at a gallop for the other side of the steppe. There Igor set up his tent and he and his beloved Alène lived happily together for many years.

Basile and the Winged Dragon

In the mountains of the Altai there arrived one day, from no one knew where, a monstrous and terrifying dragon. It was hoped that he would fly away elsewhere since he had such enormous wings; but he chose to live in a dark cave above Lake Kobdo, and he slept there for seven years. And then one day thunder awakened him, and he was very hungry!

Tchoukch the dragon — that was his name — started to scream louder than the sorceress, Baba-Yaga, louder than Tchoudo-Youdo, the monster with six heads, louder than the ogre, Almyss.

> It is I, Tchoukch the dragon!
> Someone better bring me my ration!
> Someone better come to feed me!

> Each day I must devour an ox, a cow,
>   or thirty-six chickens.
> He who comes to feed me shall live.
> He who forgets me I will eat up whole!

Everyone heard him down below, and it was the beginning of great misery in the village of Kobdo at the edge of the lake. The people were so frightened that every day they left great quantities of food near the dragon's cave, in order not to be devoured themselves.

But it was never enough, and every day they had to bring more if they did not want to hear Tchoukch the dragon cry out louder than Baba-Yaga, louder than Tchoudo-Youdo, louder than the ogre, Almyss.

> Here I am, Tchoukch the dragon!
> Someone better bring me my ration on the hour!
> He who forgets me,
> I will devour!

Soon the people of Kobdo were aware that there was no longer anything left for them. They had given him everything! They knew that the horrible winged dragon, who no longer had anything to eat either, was probably getting ready to leave the cave and come down to the village to carry off men, women, and children to his lair.

History does not say just who Basile was, nor at what moment he arrived in the village, but they are still telling about his great deed!

Basile did not wait for the inhabitants of the village to be devoured. He decided to go to Tchoukch the dragon and negotiate with him. He wound a long belt around his waist, took an enormous thick stick, and went up the path that led to the dragon's cave.

When the dragon saw the man arrive, he was astonished!

"Who are you? And what did you come to do here with your little stick that's worth nothing at all?"

"I am Basile of the village of Kobdo and I come to kill you, Tchoukch the dragon!"

"Kill me! You would do better to flee and as quickly as possible; for if I start to blow, you will find yourself three versts from here with your little stick!"

Basile started to laugh and said to him, "Don't talk so much, you old monster! Better show me what you can do, and then it will be my turn. Go ahead then, blow!"

And Tchoukch the dragon blew so hard that the branches of the trees shook and all their leaves blew off. Basile fell to his knees. But he got up and burst out laughing, "Is that what you call blowing! It seems to me that you hardly blow as powerfully as a sparrow, miserable Tchoukch! Now it is my turn to show you what I can do. And since you value your eyes, I will bind them first, because if I do not, they might fall out and you would not even be able to find them!"

Saying this, he undid his belt and used it to bind the dragon's eyes. And "BANG!" he hit him so hard with his big thick stick that Tchoukch saw three hundred and thirty-six stars and heard a terrible ringing in his ears!

"Do you dare blow harder than I?" said Tchoukch the dragon when he came to his senses. "Take this band off my eyes, and let's try something else now. Which one of us can reduce a stone to dust faster?"

The dragon took a stone from a barrel and squeezed it so hard between his huge paws that clouds of dust were raised. "I can do that even better!" exclaimed Basile. "Could you make water flow from this stone?"

Hearing this, the dragon began to believe that Basile was really stronger than he. Tchoukch looked at the thick stick. It was small, to be sure, but what if the man knew how to use it with all the strength he boasted about? Then Tchoukch the dragon softened his voice and said, "Now that you are here, ask me whatever you wish, and I will give it to you."

Basile thought for a moment of all the miserable inhabitants of the village who might die of hunger and fear because of the wicked dragon. He thought also about the dragon's huge wings which he could certainly use to leave the country. Basile thought about many things he could ask for.

But then he had a better idea.

"I have need of nothing, absolutely nothing!" he finally said to Tchoukch. "I have everything that I need at home, and much more than you possess!"

"Come, now," answered the dragon. "I do not believe you. You don't seem to be as rich as all that!"

"If you do not believe me, come home with me to see!"

"If you have a lot to eat there, I'll come!" answered the dragon without ceremony, "for I am beginning to be very hungry!"

And so the two left together, the dragon dragging his scales on the ground and Basile walking beside him.

On the road, the dragon called out, "Catch me an ox, since you are so strong! The two of us will eat it."

Basile went off into the prairie where some cattle were grazing. He went up to a little grove of birch trees and started to tear off the bark of the trees in order to weave a strong rope.

The dragon waited and waited for his ox, but nothing came! At last he called to Basile in a loud voice, "Where is my ox? Why are you taking so long? I already told you that I am very hungry!"

"I know that very well! That is why I am making a rope to catch five oxen at once."

"Why five? One would be more than enough!"

"Good," said Basile. "Then you do not have the appetite that I thought you had." He took an ox and dragged it up to the dragon's jaw.

"I would prefer to have it cooked," said the dragon. "Go get me some wood. We are going to grill it!"

Basile went into the forest, sat down under an oak tree, and started to smoke.

The dragon waited and waited for his wood, but none came. Finally he called to Basile in a loud voice, "Where is my wood? Why are you taking so long to get it? I have already told you that I am very hungry and that I want to grill my ox!"

"I want to bring you ten oak trees for firewood and I am looking for the biggest ones!"

"Come back!" screamed the dragon. "One oak tree is enough!" And he himself pulled an enormous oak tree out of the ground. Then he put the ox on the fire to grill and invited Basile to share it with him.

"Eat it yourself," answered Basile. "I will eat when I get home this evening. My wife is preparing twelve braised oxen for my supper. Your ox would only be a mouthful for me."

The dragon enjoyed his ox all by himself, and then they continued on their way.

Before long they were only half a verst from the cabin where Basile and his family lived. His children joyfully ran up to him and began to cry out, "Here's papa! He's come back! He has killed the dragon!" They did not immediately notice the dragon who, his belly too full, dragged behind a little.

"What are they saying?" asked Tchoukch. "My scales make so much noise, I do not hear very well. I think they are talking about me."

"They are saying that they are happy I brought you back, for they have already devoured ten braised oxen and now they are going to eat you!"

The frightened dragon wanted to flee, but his too round and too full stomach made him roll to the bottom of the hill at such a speed that he was unable to stop. He plunged directly into Lake Kobdo where he sunk like a rock!

They say that his carcass is still there to this day.